Decoding Private Markets: The Math Wizards Revolutionizing Wall Street

The Enigma of Private Markets

Private markets have long been a world of mystery—an exclusive club where vast fortunes are made, yet few truly understand the rules of the game. Private equity firms operate behind closed doors, moving billions of dollars with strategies and deals that can reshape entire industries. Despite their enormous influence, private markets remain frustratingly opaque, a puzzle even for the most seasoned investors.

In 2023, the private equity industry oversaw $10.6 trillion in assets, a staggering figure that underscores its critical role in the global economy. By 2033, experts predict this number will surpass $25 trillion. Behind this exponential growth lies a pressing question: How do we know if these investments are successful? For years, that question has been surprisingly difficult to answer.

Unlike public markets, where stock prices and financial disclosures provide clear indicators of performance, private markets exist in a shadowy realm of subjective valuations and incomplete data. Investors—from massive pension funds to sovereign wealth funds—are often left with limited tools to measure returns and evaluate risks. For those tasked with managing billions, the stakes couldn't be higher.

Enter the math wizards. People like Barry Griffiths, a brilliant and unconventional quantitative analyst, are changing the way Wall Street thinks about private markets. Griffiths leads a team of analysts who are reimagining how private equity and venture capital performance is measured, developing new methods that promise greater transparency and accuracy. His groundbreaking work is already reshaping the industry, challenging long-held assumptions, and offering a glimpse into the future of financial analytics.

Griffiths' journey into this specialized field began with a startling realization: The traditional tools of the trade were deeply flawed. For decades, the industry relied heavily on Internal Rate of Return (IRR) as the gold standard for measuring success. But as Griffiths dove deeper into the data, he uncovered major limitations in IRR. It was, in his words, "like using a yardstick to measure the ocean—totally inadequate."

His solution? A new approach called "direct alpha." This method evaluates private market cash flows against public equity benchmarks, providing a clearer, more objective view of performance. Unlike IRR, which can be skewed by the timing of cash flows, direct alpha levels the playing field and offers a consistent frame of reference. For major investors demanding accountability, this innovation has been transformative.

But this story isn't just about numbers and formulas. It's about the people who inhabit the high-stakes world of private markets— investors, analysts, and entrepreneurs whose decisions ripple across economies and industries. Private equity isn't just a financial abstraction; it's a force that powers innovation, funds groundbreaking ideas, and impacts the lives of millions. At the same time, it raises ethical questions about wealth concentration, corporate influence, and societal responsibility.

This book takes readers on a journey through the fascinating intersection of mathematics, finance, and human ambition. It follows Barry Griffiths and a new generation of quantitative analysts as they demystify private markets, unlocking insights once thought unattainable. Along the way, we'll explore the tools they use, the challenges they face, and the implications of their work.

Whether you're an investor, a curious observer, or someone interested in how financial markets shape the world around us, this book will illuminate a hidden world. It's a story of innovation and determination, of how math wizards are rewriting the rules of Wall Street's most secretive and influential industry.

Wall Street's Best-Kept Secrets

Private equity markets have always been a paradox—one of the most profitable arenas on Wall Street yet also one of the least understood. Unlike the stock market, where prices and performance metrics are readily available, private markets thrive on secrecy. Deals are made behind closed doors, and the true value of investments often remains hidden from view. For decades, this opacity has been both a feature and a flaw, enticing investors with the promise of exceptional returns but leaving them with few tools to measure success.

The scale of the industry is staggering. By 2023, private equity had grown into a $10.6 trillion behemoth, a figure expected to more than double to $25.1 trillion within a decade. This explosive growth is reshaping the financial landscape, yet a fundamental question looms: How do we know if private equity is delivering on its promises?

Historically, the industry relied on a handful of metrics to assess performance, with Internal Rate of Return (IRR) as the undisputed standard. IRR was easy to calculate, widely understood, and— perhaps most importantly—sufficient for an era when private equity was a niche market. But as the industry scaled and its investor base evolved, cracks began to show in this trusted tool.

The problem with IRR, as critics like Barry Griffiths point out, is that it often obscures more than it reveals. A skilled fund manager can manipulate IRR by returning capital early in the investment's lifecycle, creating an illusion of strong performance even if the overall returns are mediocre. For institutional investors managing billions of dollars on behalf of retirees and taxpayers, this lack of clarity is no longer acceptable.

Barry Griffiths is no ordinary critic. A mathematician by training and a Wall Street veteran, Griffiths has become one of the leading voices in the push to modernize how private markets are measured. Early in his career, he worked in hedge funds, where quantitative analysis had already revolutionized trading strategies. But private equity intrigued him precisely because it hadn't yet been subjected to the same level of mathematical rigor. "It was a black box," he recalls. "No one was asking the hard questions about how performance was measured."

Griffiths wasn't alone in sensing an opportunity. The rise of quantitative analysis, or "quant" strategies, in finance was already reshaping public markets. Armed with advanced algorithms and computational power, these analysts were uncovering patterns and insights that had eluded traditional investors. Yet private markets remained resistant to this wave of innovation, partly because of their inherent complexity and partly because of the industry's preference for secrecy.

Griffiths' breakthrough came when he developed a metric known as "direct alpha." Unlike IRR, which can be skewed by the timing of cash flows, direct alpha compares private market performance to public equity benchmarks. This apples-to-apples approach provides a clearer picture of how private equity stacks up against more traditional investments, stripping away many of the distortions that had plagued earlier metrics.

The impact of this innovation was profound. When Norway's $1.8 trillion sovereign wealth fund adopted direct alpha as its preferred metric for evaluating private equity investments, it sent shockwaves through the industry. Other major investors, from pension plans to university endowments, began to take notice. For the first time, private equity's performance could be assessed with the same level of rigor as public market investments.

But not everyone welcomed the change. For many private equity firms, the lack of transparency was a feature, not a bug. Greater scrutiny could expose weaknesses in their strategies, challenge their fee structures, and force them to justify their returns in ways they hadn't before. Even among investors, there was resistance. Some worried that focusing too much on metrics like direct alpha could oversimplify the nuanced and long-term nature of private equity investing.

Despite these hurdles, the momentum was undeniable. As private equity continued its march toward $25 trillion in assets under management, the demand for better analytics only grew. Investors were no longer content with vague assurances of strong performance. They wanted data, accountability, and a clearer understanding of the risks and rewards involved.

Griffiths and his team were at the forefront of this transformation, using advanced tools like machine learning and predictive modeling to uncover hidden patterns in private market data. Their work was part science, part art—a blend of mathematical precision and intuitive insight that was reshaping how Wall Street viewed private equity.

"The numbers don't lie," Griffiths often said, "but they don't tell the whole story either." For him, the goal wasn't just to create better metrics but to foster a deeper understanding of what private equity could achieve. His work wasn't about tearing down the industry but about building a stronger, more transparent foundation for its future.

As the private equity market evolves, its impact on the broader economy will only grow. From funding groundbreaking startups to restructuring struggling businesses, these investments touch nearly every aspect of modern life. Yet for all its influence, private equity remains a mystery to most people—a world of immense complexity hidden behind the allure of high returns.

In the chapters ahead, we'll explore how Barry Griffiths and a new generation of math wizards are pulling back the curtain on private markets. We'll look at the tools they use, the challenges they face, and the broader implications of their work. More than just a story about numbers, this is a story about the future of finance—and the people who are rewriting its rules.

The Rise of the Quants

For decades, the term "quant" evoked images of mathematically gifted analysts revolutionizing public markets. In the 1980s and 1990s, these quantitative thinkers transformed trading by using sophisticated algorithms to uncover patterns that escaped the traditional investor's eye. By the 2000s, quants had become an indispensable part of Wall Street, driving innovations in high-frequency trading, portfolio management, and risk assessment.

Yet, even as quants took public markets by storm, private equity remained largely untouched by their analytical tools. Unlike the transparency of public markets, private equity operated in a world of opacity, where data was scarce, valuations subjective, and transactions uniquely structured. For a long time, this murkiness shielded private equity from the wave of data-driven disruption. But by the mid-2010s, as the industry swelled to manage trillions in assets, the pressure to innovate became impossible to ignore.

This was the moment when quants set their sights on private equity. And for analysts like Barry Griffiths, the challenge presented an irresistible frontier.

Breaking Into the Black Box

Barry Griffiths was no stranger to complex financial systems. A mathematician by training, he had spent years honing his skills in hedge funds, where quantitative analysis was already a cornerstone of success. But while public markets teemed with clean, standardized data, private equity was a different beast entirely.

"It was like trying to navigate a labyrinth without a map," Griffiths recalls. "The data was messy, the benchmarks unreliable, and the methods for measuring success were deeply flawed."

Private equity's opacity was both its appeal and its Achilles' heel. For years, investors had relied on Internal Rate of Return (IRR) to evaluate performance. On the surface, IRR appeared simple: it calculated the profitability of an investment based on its cash flows and the time taken to generate returns. But Griffiths soon realized that IRR had critical shortcomings. Its sensitivity to the timing of cash flows made it easy to manipulate, and it offered little insight into the actual risks taken to achieve those returns.

As private equity ballooned into a $10.6 trillion industry, these limitations became glaring. Investors, especially large institutions like pension funds and sovereign wealth funds, began demanding more robust metrics to assess performance. For Griffiths, this presented an opportunity to bring the rigor of quantitative analysis into a space that had long resisted it.

The Direct Alpha Revolution

Griffiths' most significant breakthrough came in the form of a new metric: direct alpha. Unlike IRR, which could be distorted by cash flow timing, direct alpha provided an objective comparison between private market returns and public equity benchmarks. The idea was simple but powerful: measure private equity's performance in terms of how much additional return it generated compared to publicly traded investments.

"Direct alpha strips away the noise," Griffiths explains. "It gives you a clear, unvarnished look at how private equity stacks up against other opportunities."

The impact of this innovation was immediate. Large institutional investors, including Norway's $1.8 trillion sovereign wealth fund and Japan's $1.6 trillion Government Pension Investment Fund, adopted direct alpha as a key metric for evaluating private equity. These organizations, responsible for managing vast pools of capital, saw direct alpha as a way to hold fund managers accountable and ensure their investments were truly delivering value.

Yet, the adoption of direct alpha wasn't without resistance. For many private equity firms, the lack of transparency had long been a feature, not a bug. Greater scrutiny threatened to expose weaknesses in their strategies and challenge their lucrative fee structures. Griffiths faced skepticism not only from fund managers but also from investors wary of abandoning the familiarity of IRR.

Still, the momentum was undeniable. As more institutions embraced direct alpha, the pressure on private equity firms to adapt intensified. For Griffiths, this was a validation of years of hard work—but it was also just the beginning.

The Role of Machine Learning

While direct alpha was a game changer, it was only one piece of the puzzle. Griffiths and his team began exploring advanced techniques like machine learning to analyze the mountains of data generated by private markets. These algorithms could identify patterns and relationships that even the most experienced analysts might miss, offering new insights into risk, performance, and opportunity.

One application involved predicting future cash flows based on historical data. By analyzing thousands of transactions across different sectors and geographies, Griffiths' models could forecast the likelihood of success for individual investments. Another focused on risk assessment, identifying hidden vulnerabilities in portfolios that traditional methods often overlooked.

But while the potential of machine learning was enormous, it also came with challenges. Private equity data was notoriously incomplete, and models were only as good as the information fed into them. Griffiths was keenly aware of these limitations. "The goal isn't to replace human judgment," he says. "It's to augment it. The best decisions come from combining intuition with data-driven insights."

A Cultural Shift

The rise of the quants marked a cultural shift in private equity. For decades, the industry had operated on relationships and instinct—a world where deals were often sealed over dinner rather than spreadsheets. The quants brought a new level of objectivity, challenging long-held assumptions and forcing firms to back up their claims with hard data.

This transition wasn't always smooth. Traditional fund managers often viewed quants with suspicion, fearing that their models oversimplified the complexities of private equity investing. But as firms that embraced analytics began outperforming their peers, attitudes started to change.

Griffiths, for his part, saw himself as a bridge between these two worlds. "Numbers tell part of the story, but not the whole story," he says. "The art of investing is just as important as the science. What we're trying to do is bring the two together."

Looking Ahead

As private equity marches toward $25 trillion in assets under management, the role of analytics will only grow. New tools and techniques are emerging every year, from real-time data analysis to simulations that model complex investment scenarios. For investors, these advances hold the promise of better insights, smarter decisions, and higher returns.

Yet the rise of the quants also raises important questions. How do we balance data with intuition? What happens when models fail to account for unforeseen events? And how do we ensure that the drive for transparency doesn't stifle the creativity and risk-taking that have long defined private equity?

For Barry Griffiths, these questions are as much about philosophy as they are about finance. "Private equity is evolving," he says. "But at its core, it's still about people—about understanding their ambitions, their fears, and their potential. Data can guide us, but it's the human element that will always make this industry what it is."

Challenges in Measuring Private Market Performance

Private markets have always carried an air of exclusivity, their mystique amplified by their inaccessibility. Investors are drawn to their potential for outsized returns, but with great promise comes the ever-present challenge: How do you measure success in a world defined by opacity? For decades, this question has haunted the industry, creating a paradox where vast amounts of wealth are at stake, yet the tools to evaluate performance remain imperfect.

Unlike public markets, private markets operate in the shadows. Deals are private, valuations are often speculative, and performance metrics can feel more like educated guesses than hard facts. For institutional investors managing trillions of dollars, this lack of transparency is more than just inconvenient—it's risky.

Economic Pressures and a Need for Clarity

The fragility of private market performance metrics became glaringly obvious in 2023, as shifting economic conditions began to strain the system. Rising borrowing costs cut into returns, making it harder for firms to offload investments profitably. Regulatory scrutiny added pressure, forcing fund managers to justify valuations that once went unquestioned.

For Barry Griffiths, these challenges underscored an urgent reality: the industry's traditional methods for measuring performance were no longer enough. "When you're managing billions, you need to know where you stand," Griffiths explains. "And right now, too many people are flying blind."

The core of the problem lay in the tools the industry had long relied on. Metrics like Internal Rate of Return (IRR) had been used for decades to evaluate private equity investments. IRR offered a straightforward way to calculate an investment's annualized return over time, making it a favorite of fund managers and investors alike. But as Griffiths discovered early in his career, IRR came with significant flaws.

The Illusions of IRR

One of the most persistent criticisms of IRR is its susceptibility to manipulation. Because the calculation places heavy emphasis on the timing of cash flows, fund managers can inflate IRR by returning capital to investors early—even if the overall investment underperforms. This creates what Griffiths calls "a mirage of success," where impressive-looking IRRs mask deeper issues within a portfolio.

Griffiths recalls a moment early in his career that brought this problem into sharp focus. "We had two funds on paper that looked identical—they both boasted IRRs of around 15%. But when we dug into the numbers, one fund had achieved that return by taking on significantly more risk, while the other had a more stable, long-term strategy. Yet, IRR didn't reflect that difference."

The reliance on IRR also created blind spots when it came to assessing risk. Two funds with the same IRR could have wildly different risk profiles, yet investors had little means of distinguishing between them. For institutional investors—particularly pension funds and sovereign wealth funds managing the livelihoods of millions—this lack of clarity was becoming untenable.

The Birth of Direct Alpha

Griffiths' solution to these issues was the development of a new metric: direct alpha. Where IRR fell short, direct alpha provided a clearer and more reliable measure of performance by comparing private market returns to public equity benchmarks. This method contextualized private equity performance, offering investors a way to see how their returns stacked up against the broader market.

"Direct alpha doesn't just measure returns," Griffiths explains. "It measures value. It asks the question: Is this investment worth the risks you're taking compared to what you could achieve elsewhere?"

The introduction of direct alpha marked a turning point. Large institutions like Norway's $1.8 trillion sovereign wealth fund quickly adopted the metric, setting a new standard for transparency and accountability. For fund managers, this shift was both a challenge and an opportunity. While it forced them to confront weaknesses in their strategies, it also gave them a powerful tool to communicate the real value of their investments to stakeholders.

Analytics in the Spotlight

Direct alpha was a critical innovation, but it was only part of the solution. For Griffiths and his team, the next step was leveraging advanced analytics to make sense of the vast, unstructured data that defined private markets. Machine learning, in particular, emerged as a game-changing tool, capable of uncovering patterns and insights that traditional analysis often missed.

One early success came from using machine learning to predict cash flows. By analyzing historical data from thousands of private equity transactions, Griffiths' models were able to forecast future returns with surprising accuracy. In another instance, machine learning helped a major pension fund identify previously overlooked risks in its portfolio, preventing a potentially disastrous investment.

Yet, for all its promise, machine learning also highlighted the limits of private market data. Unlike public markets, where data is standardized and widely available, private markets often operate with incomplete or inconsistent information. This made it difficult to build models that were both reliable and actionable.

Griffiths is quick to point out that analytics are not a panacea. "The models can only take you so far," he says. "They're a tool, not a replacement for judgment. The best outcomes come from combining data-driven insights with experience and intuition."

A New Standard for Private Markets

As private markets grow—on track to surpass $25 trillion in assets by 2033—the demand for better performance metrics and analytics is only intensifying. Investors are no longer content with vague assurances of strong returns. They want tools that provide transparency, accountability, and a deeper understanding of both risks and rewards.

Griffiths views this shift as a natural evolution. "Private equity is maturing," he says. "And with that maturity comes a higher standard of scrutiny. Investors want to know not just that their money is growing, but how and why it's growing."

This maturation has not been without its challenges. Many in the industry remain resistant to change, clinging to traditional metrics like IRR out of familiarity or convenience. Others worry that the push for transparency could stifle innovation or discourage risk-taking. For Griffiths, these concerns are valid but not insurmountable.

"The goal isn't to dismantle what's worked in the past," he explains. "It's to build on it—to create a system that's not only more transparent but also more adaptable to the complexities of modern private markets."

Looking Ahead

The challenges of measuring private market performance are far from resolved, but progress is undeniable. Tools like direct alpha and machine learning are pushing the industry toward greater transparency and accountability, while also opening up new possibilities for understanding and managing risk. For investors, these advances represent a powerful step forward, offering the clarity they need to make smarter decisions.

At the same time, the journey is just beginning. Questions remain about how to handle incomplete data, how to balance short-term performance with long-term goals, and how to ensure that analytics serve as a complement to human expertise rather than a replacement. For Barry Griffiths and his peers, these challenges are less an obstacle than an opportunity—a chance to shape the future of private equity.

"Private markets will always be complex," Griffiths says. "But complexity doesn't have to mean confusion. The more we understand, the better we can navigate this space—and the more value we can create for everyone involved."

Current Market Pressures and Valuation Challenges

Private equity has always existed in a delicate balance between promise and complexity. While the sector offers investors the potential for extraordinary returns, its lack of transparency and inherent risk make it one of the most challenging areas of finance. In 2023, that balance was tested like never before. Rising interest rates, an unpredictable global economy, and growing regulatory scrutiny created a cascade of pressures that pushed fund managers to adapt— or risk being left behind.

At the heart of these challenges lay the question of valuation. How do you measure the value of private investments when the data is incomplete, benchmarks are inconsistent, and the rules are always shifting? For the firms managing trillions of dollars and the investors relying on their judgment, the stakes couldn't be higher.

The Weight of Rising Rates

One of the most immediate and visible pressures on private equity in 2023 was the rise in borrowing costs. For years, the industry thrived in an environment of low interest rates, where cheap debt allowed firms to finance acquisitions, restructure companies, and boost returns. But as central banks around the world tightened monetary policy to combat inflation, that dynamic began to unravel.

Deals that once penciled out as lucrative suddenly looked precarious as financing costs ate into profit margins. Leveraged buyouts, a staple of private equity strategy, became significantly harder to justify under the weight of higher rates. For some firms, the math simply stopped working. Instead of selling portfolio companies and returning capital to investors, they were forced to hold onto assets longer, waiting for a more favorable market.

"Debt has always been the secret weapon of private equity," says Barry Griffiths. "It amplifies returns when the environment is right.

But when borrowing gets expensive, it becomes a weight around your neck."

The Liquidity Crunch

The rise in borrowing costs also exacerbated one of private equity's long-standing vulnerabilities: liquidity—or the lack thereof. Unlike public markets, where assets can be traded quickly, private investments are often locked up for years. This illiquidity is usually an accepted part of the deal, but in a tough economic environment, it can become a serious problem.

In 2023, this issue came to a head as firms struggled to find buyers for portfolio companies. IPO markets had slowed to a crawl, and potential acquirers were increasingly wary, driving down valuations. For many fund managers, the result was a frustrating stalemate: they couldn't sell their holdings at acceptable prices, nor could they justify keeping them indefinitely.

The delays created ripple effects throughout the industry. Institutional investors, including pension funds and endowments, were forced to recalibrate their expectations for cash returns. Meanwhile, fund managers faced mounting pressure to demonstrate that their investments were still viable.

Valuations Under Fire

Amid these challenges, the spotlight turned to valuations—a cornerstone of private equity that had always been more art than science. Unlike publicly traded stocks, whose prices are determined by the open market, private equity valuations rely on a mix of market trends, financial projections, and subjective judgments by fund managers. While this flexibility has historically been seen as an advantage, it also leaves valuations open to skepticism.

In 2023, as economic pressures mounted, regulators began taking a harder look at how firms were valuing their assets. Were managers inflating valuations to maintain appearances, or were they appropriately adjusting for market conditions? Were underperforming assets being marked down, or were they quietly left on the books at overly optimistic prices?

For Griffiths, these questions struck at the heart of private equity's credibility. "Investors aren't just trusting you with their money," he says. "They're trusting you to be honest about what that money is worth. And right now, too many firms are falling short of that standard."

Analytics to the Rescue

To address these challenges, many firms turned to advanced analytics, hoping to bring greater precision and objectivity to their valuation processes. Tools like machine learning and predictive modeling offered a way to analyze vast amounts of data, identify hidden patterns, and project future outcomes with greater accuracy.

Griffiths and his team were among the leaders in this effort. By leveraging machine learning, they were able to assess thousands of private equity transactions, uncovering insights that traditional methods had missed. For example, their models identified specific economic indicators that consistently correlated with valuation declines, giving firms an early warning system for potential problems.

"Data doesn't lie," Griffiths says. "If you know how to read it, it can tell you a lot about where the risks are—and where the opportunities might be."

But while advanced analytics provided valuable insights, they weren't without limitations. Private equity data remained inconsistent and incomplete, making it difficult to build models that were entirely reliable. And, as Griffiths points out, analytics alone can't replace human judgment. "The numbers are a tool," he says. "They help you see the picture, but it's up to you to interpret what it means."

The Role of Regulation

As valuation practices came under scrutiny, regulators began implementing stricter requirements for transparency. Firms were now expected to provide more detailed disclosures about how they arrived at their valuations, forcing some to confront uncomfortable truths about their internal processes.

For many fund managers, this shift was seen as a burden. But for others, it represented an opportunity to rebuild trust with investors. "Regulation doesn't have to be the enemy," Griffiths argues. "If you're doing things the right way, transparency should be your ally."

Balancing Short-Term Pressures with Long-Term Vision

The pressures of 2023 forced private equity firms to walk a tightrope between short-term realities and long-term goals. On one hand, investors demanded immediate answers—strong valuations, steady cash returns, and assurances that their capital was safe. On the other, the very nature of private equity requires patience and a willingness to weather short-term volatility for long-term rewards.

Griffiths believes that striking this balance is critical to the industry's future. "Private equity isn't about quick wins," he says. "It's about creating real value over time. That's what we need to keep our focus on, even when the market is throwing curveballs."

The Road Ahead

The pressures of 2023 marked a turning point for private equity. Rising borrowing costs, liquidity challenges, and heightened scrutiny on valuations forced the industry to confront its vulnerabilities. Yet, these same pressures also created an opportunity for innovation, pushing firms to adopt better tools, refine their strategies, and embrace a new standard of transparency.

For Griffiths, the lessons of this moment are clear. "Every challenge is an opportunity to improve," he says. "The firms that adapt to these changes—the ones that embrace analytics, transparency, and smarter valuation methods—are the ones that will lead the industry forward."

As private equity continues to evolve, the question isn't whether the industry can adapt but how quickly it can rise to meet the moment. For investors, the promise of a more transparent and accountable future is within reach. And for fund managers, the opportunity to redefine what success looks like in private markets has never been greater.

Traditional Performance Metrics and Their Limitations

For decades, the private equity industry relied on a familiar set of metrics to assess performance. Chief among them was the Internal Rate of Return (IRR), a calculation so entrenched in the industry that many investors equated it with success. Alongside IRR, measures like Multiple on Invested Capital (MOIC) rounded out the tools fund managers used to gauge profitability. For a time, these metrics seemed to suffice. But as private equity grew in size, complexity, and influence, their flaws became impossible to ignore.

IRR and MOIC were developed in an era when private markets were simpler, smaller, and less interconnected with the broader financial system. Today, with private equity managing trillions of dollars in assets and institutional investors demanding higher standards of accountability, the limitations of these metrics are more glaring than ever.

The Mirage of IRR

At first glance, IRR seems like an ideal measure of success. It calculates the annualized rate of return on an investment, taking into account the timing of cash flows. Its simplicity makes it an easy number to tout to investors, and it provides a clear way to compare investments across different funds or firms.

But IRR has a darker side. Because it is highly sensitive to the timing of cash flows, fund managers can manipulate it to appear more favorable than it actually is. For example, returning a portion of capital to investors early in the life of a fund can dramatically inflate the IRR, even if the fund underperforms over its entire lifespan. This creates what Barry Griffiths calls "a mirage of success."

"I've seen funds with IRRs that looked incredible on paper," Griffiths says, "but when you really dug into the numbers, the story didn't hold up. The return might have come from one lucky exit or a well-timed distribution, while the rest of the portfolio languished."

Another shortcoming of IRR is its inability to account for scale. A small investment that generates a high IRR might look impressive, but if it contributes only a fraction of the overall returns in a large portfolio, its impact is negligible. For institutional investors managing billions of dollars, absolute returns often matter more than percentages.

The Flaws of MOIC

To complement IRR, private equity managers often rely on Multiple on Invested Capital (MOIC), which measures the total value of an investment—both realized and unrealized—divided by the amount of capital invested. MOIC is often praised for its simplicity and its ability to show the full value of an investment over time.

However, MOIC has its own pitfalls. Unlike IRR, it does not account for the time value of money, making it hard to compare investments with different durations. A fund that delivers a 2x MOIC over five years may be less attractive than one that achieves the same multiple in three, but MOIC doesn't make that distinction.

MOIC also suffers from subjectivity, particularly when it includes unrealized gains. Because unrealized gains are based on valuations of assets that haven't yet been sold, they can be influenced by overly optimistic assumptions or market trends that may not hold. In a frothy market, inflated valuations can make MOIC look far more favorable than it truly is.

"MOIC is useful, but it has to be taken with a grain of salt," Griffiths explains. "It's only as reliable as the assumptions underlying it. And in this industry, assumptions can vary wildly."

The Cost of Incomplete Metrics

The reliance on IRR and MOIC isn't just a technical issue—it shapes behavior. Fund managers, eager to present appealing numbers to investors, may prioritize short-term gains or take unnecessary risks to boost metrics. This focus can distort decision-making, leading to suboptimal outcomes for investors in the long run.

For institutional investors, the consequences are even more pronounced. Pension funds, endowments, and sovereign wealth funds rely on private equity to provide consistent returns that align with their long-term goals. When those returns are measured with tools that fail to account for risk, timing, or scale, the picture they see is incomplete—and sometimes misleading.

The Push for Better Tools

Recognizing the limitations of traditional metrics, forward-thinking fund managers and investors are calling for better tools to evaluate performance. For Griffiths, this is more than just an academic exercise—it's essential for the industry's survival.

"The private equity market has grown beyond the point where we can rely on simplistic metrics," he says. "We need measures that reflect the complexities of today's investments."

One promising alternative is direct alpha, a metric Griffiths helped develop. Unlike IRR, direct alpha compares private equity returns to public equity benchmarks, offering a clearer and more objective measure of success. By contextualizing private equity performance within the broader market, direct alpha helps investors determine whether their capital is being deployed effectively.

Another innovation is the use of risk-adjusted metrics, which factor in the volatility and uncertainty associated with private equity investments. These tools provide a more nuanced view of performance, helping investors make smarter decisions about where to allocate their capital.

A Cultural Shift

The move toward better metrics reflects a broader cultural shift in private equity. For years, the industry operated on a mix of intuition, relationships, and opaque reporting. But as private equity has become more institutionalized, the demand for transparency and accountability has reshaped the landscape.

Griffiths sees this shift as inevitable—and ultimately beneficial. "The days of relying on trust and charisma are over," he says. "Investors want data. They want proof. And they're right to ask for it."

Not everyone welcomes this change. Some fund managers argue that too much emphasis on metrics can undermine the art of investing, reducing complex decisions to simple numbers. But Griffiths believes the two approaches can coexist. "Good metrics don't replace intuition," he says. "They enhance it. They give you a foundation to build on."

The Path Forward

As private equity continues to grow, the limitations of traditional metrics like IRR and MOIC will only become more apparent. For fund managers and investors alike, the challenge is clear: find better ways to measure success, or risk falling behind in an increasingly competitive landscape.

Griffiths is optimistic about the future. "We're at a turning point," he says. "The tools we develop now will define the next era of private equity. If we can get it right, we'll not only deliver better returns but also build an industry that's more transparent, accountable, and sustainable."

The stakes are high, but so are the opportunities. For those willing to embrace change, the future of private equity holds immense promise—and the chance to rewrite the rules of an industry poised to shape the global economy for decades to come.

The Need for Advanced Analytics

The private equity industry is undergoing a fundamental shift. As the size and complexity of the market have grown, the traditional tools for measuring success and managing risk are no longer enough. Advanced analytics, once a niche concept in finance, is rapidly becoming essential. These sophisticated tools and techniques are helping fund managers and investors navigate an increasingly complex landscape, uncovering insights that were previously out of reach.

The need for advanced analytics isn't just a response to the shortcomings of traditional metrics like IRR or MOIC. It reflects a broader change in the nature of private equity itself. Deals are larger, portfolios more diverse, and market conditions more volatile than ever. For those managing trillions of dollars in assets, the ability to analyze data effectively has become a critical competitive advantage.

Private Markets: A Complex and Evolving Landscape

Today's private equity market bears little resemblance to the industry of a few decades ago. What was once a niche investment strategy has grown into a $10.6 trillion behemoth. As the market has expanded, so too has its complexity. Portfolios now span industries, geographies, and asset classes, creating a web of interconnected variables that fund managers must untangle to deliver returns.

At the heart of this complexity is the explosion of data. Every transaction, every portfolio company, and every market event generates a flood of information. But this data is often unstructured, fragmented, and difficult to interpret. Traditional analysis methods, which rely on simplified models and limited datasets, are struggling to keep up.

"Data has always been the foundation of good decision-making," says Barry Griffiths, one of the pioneers of analytics in private equity. "But in today's world, it's not just about having data—it's about knowing how to extract meaning from it. That's where advanced analytics makes the difference."

What Advanced Analytics Brings to the Table

Advanced analytics isn't just about crunching numbers faster. It's about uncovering patterns, making predictions, and supporting better decisions. By combining statistical modeling, machine learning, and computational power, advanced analytics provides a range of tools that are transforming the way private equity operates.

1. **Sharper Performance Metrics**
   Advanced analytics addresses the limitations of traditional metrics by providing more nuanced and accurate measures of performance. Risk-adjusted metrics, for example, account for the volatility and uncertainty inherent in private markets, offering a clearer picture of how returns are achieved.
2. **Proactive Risk Management**
   Machine learning algorithms can analyze historical data to identify correlations and anticipate risks. This might involve spotting early warning signs of underperformance in a

portfolio company or identifying macroeconomic trends that could affect valuations.

3. **Enhanced Valuation Models**
   One of private equity's long-standing challenges has been valuing assets accurately. Predictive modeling can use historical transaction data to estimate fair values, providing fund managers with more reliable benchmarks and reducing the subjectivity of traditional methods.

4. **Portfolio Optimization**
   With the ability to process massive datasets, advanced analytics helps fund managers identify opportunities for improving portfolio performance, from reallocating resources to restructuring underperforming assets.

The Role of Machine Learning

Machine learning has emerged as one of the most transformative tools in advanced analytics. Unlike traditional models, which rely on fixed assumptions, machine learning algorithms adapt and improve as they process more data. This makes them particularly well-suited to the dynamic and often unpredictable world of private equity.

For Griffiths and his team, machine learning is a cornerstone of their approach. By analyzing thousands of historical transactions, their algorithms can identify patterns that traditional methods miss. In one case, their models flagged early warning signs of trouble in a portfolio company, allowing the fund to intervene and mitigate losses before they escalated.

"Machine learning isn't magic," Griffiths explains. "It's not going to tell you what's going to happen with absolute certainty. But it gives you insights you wouldn't have seen otherwise. It helps you make better decisions."

Challenges in Adopting Advanced Analytics

While the benefits of advanced analytics are clear, its adoption in private equity has not been without challenges. One of the biggest hurdles is the quality of the data itself. Unlike public markets, where information is standardized and widely available, private markets operate with fragmented and inconsistent datasets. This makes it difficult to build models that are both accurate and actionable.

Another challenge is cultural. Private equity has traditionally been a relationship-driven industry, where intuition and experience play a central role in decision-making. For some fund managers, the shift to data-driven approaches feels like a departure from the art of investing. Incorporating advanced analytics requires not only new tools but also a new mindset—one that values data as a complement to human judgment rather than a replacement for it.

Griffiths acknowledges these challenges but sees them as surmountable. "The technology is only as good as the people using it," he says. "You need teams that not only understand the tools but also know how to apply them in the real world."

A Competitive Imperative

Despite the obstacles, the adoption of advanced analytics is no longer optional for firms that want to stay competitive. Investors are demanding higher levels of transparency, accountability, and performance. Advanced analytics provides a way to meet those demands while also uncovering new opportunities for growth.

"The firms that invest in analytics now are positioning themselves for the future," Griffiths says. "It's not just about keeping up—it's about staying ahead."

This trend is driving a wave of innovation across the industry. Some firms are building in-house analytics teams, while others are partnering with technology providers or investing in cutting-edge data platforms. The result is a rapidly evolving landscape where the ability to leverage advanced analytics is becoming a key differentiator.

A New Era for Private Equity

As advanced analytics becomes more integrated into private equity, its impact will extend far beyond individual firms. By providing clearer insights, more accurate valuations, and better risk management, these tools have the potential to reshape the entire industry, making it more transparent, efficient, and accountable.

For Griffiths, this transformation is both exciting and daunting. "We're just starting to see what's possible," he says. "The tools we have today are powerful, but they're only going to get better. The challenge is making sure we use them responsibly and intelligently."

The future of private equity will be shaped by the firms that embrace analytics as a core part of their strategy. For fund managers and investors alike, the ability to harness these tools will be critical—not just for navigating the complexities of today's markets but for redefining the industry itself.

Direct Alpha and the Shift to Benchmarking

For much of its history, private equity has operated in its own silo, using metrics like Internal Rate of Return (IRR) to assess performance. These metrics, while effective in their time, failed to place private equity returns in the context of broader market opportunities. As the industry grew and institutional investors began demanding more sophisticated evaluations, it became clear that a new approach was needed—one that would offer both transparency and a reliable basis for comparison. That approach came in the form of direct alpha, a metric that has since revolutionized how private equity is benchmarked and understood.

Direct alpha represents more than just a technical advancement; it's a conceptual shift. By linking private equity performance to public market benchmarks, it reframes how success is measured. For investors managing billions or even trillions of dollars, this shift has been transformative, enabling them to evaluate private equity not in isolation but as part of a larger portfolio strategy.

Why Traditional Metrics Fell Short

The limitations of traditional metrics like IRR were instrumental in the rise of direct alpha. While IRR calculates the annualized return of a private equity investment, it offers no comparison to what an investor might have achieved in the public markets. This lack of benchmarking left a critical question unanswered: Were private equity investments outperforming other opportunities?

In the early days of private equity, when the industry was smaller and its returns significantly outpaced public markets, this lack of context was overlooked. But as the sector grew and its returns became more varied, investors began demanding clearer answers.

Barry Griffiths was among those pushing for change. "It's not enough to know you're making money," he explains. "Investors need to know they're making the best possible use of their capital. That means comparing private equity to the alternatives."

How Direct Alpha Works

Direct alpha addresses this need by linking private market returns to public market benchmarks. The metric compares the cash flows generated by a private equity investment to what an investor could have earned by allocating the same amount to a public equity index. This simple but powerful approach provides a clear measure of whether private equity is delivering excess returns relative to public markets.

For example, if an investor commits $10 million to a private equity fund, direct alpha evaluates how that $10 million would have performed if it had been invested in a public index, such as the S&P 500 or a sector-specific benchmark like the NASDAQ. The difference between these two outcomes is the direct alpha, offering an objective measure of whether the private equity investment added value.

"Direct alpha isn't just another number," Griffiths says. "It's a tool for understanding performance in a broader context. It lets you see not just how your private equity is performing, but how it's performing relative to the market as a whole."

The Power of Benchmarking

One of the key strengths of direct alpha is its ability to normalize performance across funds, time periods, and market conditions. Unlike IRR, which can be skewed by the timing of cash flows, direct alpha provides a consistent point of comparison that reflects the true opportunity cost of an investment.

This has been particularly valuable for institutional investors such as pension funds and sovereign wealth funds, which allocate capital across multiple asset classes. For these investors, direct alpha offers a way to determine whether their private equity portfolios are living up to expectations or whether their resources could be better deployed elsewhere.

"Direct alpha has shifted the way we think about private equity," says one institutional investor. "It's no longer just about returns in isolation. It's about returns in context—against benchmarks, against alternatives, and against what we could have achieved in public markets."

Challenges in Adoption

Despite its advantages, implementing direct alpha has not been without challenges. One of the most significant hurdles lies in selecting the appropriate benchmark. Public market performance varies widely depending on the index, sector, and geography, and choosing the wrong benchmark can lead to misleading results.

For instance, a private equity fund focused on technology might outperform a broad market index like the S&P 500 but underperform a tech-focused index like the NASDAQ. Using the S&P 500 as a benchmark in this case would provide an incomplete picture of the fund's performance.

"Choosing the right benchmark is both an art and a science," Griffiths explains. "It requires a deep understanding of the fund's strategy, its sector focus, and the market dynamics at play."

Another challenge is the data required to calculate direct alpha. Unlike public markets, where data is readily available, private equity operates with less transparency. Detailed cash flow data and market performance records are essential for calculating direct alpha, but they can be difficult to obtain—particularly for older funds or those with inconsistent reporting practices.

Adoption Among Institutional Investors

Despite these challenges, direct alpha has been embraced by some of the world's largest and most sophisticated institutional investors. Norway's $1.8 trillion sovereign wealth fund, Japan's $1.6 trillion Government Pension Investment Fund, and major pension plans like UPS have all adopted the metric as a cornerstone of their private equity evaluation processes.

For these investors, the benefits of direct alpha far outweigh the difficulties of implementation. By providing a clear, objective measure of performance, it empowers them to make more informed decisions about their allocations and ensures that private equity remains an integral part of their investment strategies.

"Direct alpha is a game-changer," Griffiths says. "It's no longer just about whether you're making money. It's about whether you're making more money than you could make elsewhere—and that's the kind of accountability investors deserve."

Implications for the Industry

The rise of direct alpha represents a broader trend toward transparency and accountability in private equity. As investors demand clearer benchmarks and more rigorous evaluations, fund managers are being forced to adapt. This shift is reshaping the industry, pushing it toward more data-driven and investor-focused practices.

Griffiths views this evolution as a positive development. "Private equity is maturing," he says. "It's becoming more professional, more transparent, and more aligned with what investors need. Direct alpha is a big part of that journey."

Looking ahead, Griffiths believes direct alpha will continue to play a pivotal role in the industry's transformation. "It's not just a metric," he says. "It's a mindset. It's about holding ourselves to a higher standard and ensuring that private equity delivers real value—not just for fund managers, but for the investors who rely on us."

Big Data and the Machine Learning Revolution in Private Equity

Private equity has always been a business built on data—poring over financial statements, scrutinizing market trends, and forecasting growth potential. For decades, much of this work relied on human intuition and traditional analytical tools. But as the industry has expanded and the volume of information available has surged, those old approaches are no longer sufficient. The advent of big data and machine learning is revolutionizing private equity, introducing new ways to extract insights, assess risks, and identify opportunities.

In a world where investment decisions can shift billions of dollars and reshape industries, leveraging the power of data has become a competitive imperative. Big data and machine learning aren't just optional tools—they're defining the next era of private equity.

The Rise of Big Data in Private Equity

Private equity firms have always dealt with data, but the scope and complexity of that data have grown exponentially. Portfolio companies now generate unprecedented streams of information, from customer behavior and operational metrics to market dynamics. On top of that, firms are tapping into external data sources like social media trends, macroeconomic indicators, and industry-specific reports to guide their strategies.

This explosion of data presents both a challenge and an opportunity. On one hand, the sheer volume can be overwhelming, making it difficult to separate meaningful patterns from the noise. On the other, it provides an unparalleled chance to uncover insights that were previously out of reach.

"Data has always been central to private equity," says Barry Griffiths, a leading voice in applying advanced analytics to the industry. "The difference today is that we have tools that allow us to extract far deeper insights from that data—and act on them in ways we couldn't before."

The Role of Machine Learning

Machine learning, a subset of artificial intelligence, is leading the charge in this transformation. Unlike traditional analytical methods, which rely on static assumptions, machine learning algorithms evolve and adapt as they process more data. This makes them particularly well-suited to the dynamic and often unpredictable nature of private equity.

Some of the most impactful applications of machine learning in private equity include:

1. **Predictive Analytics**
   Machine learning excels at analyzing historical data to predict future outcomes. Whether it's forecasting a portfolio company's revenue or identifying market trends that could affect an acquisition, predictive analytics allows fund managers to make more informed decisions.
2. **Risk Detection**
   Machine learning can uncover risks that traditional analysis might miss. By identifying subtle patterns and correlations, algorithms can flag potential red flags in a company's financials or market environment, giving managers the chance to address issues early.
3. **Streamlined Deal Sourcing**
   In a crowded market, finding the right deal is critical. Machine learning can scan vast datasets to identify potential investment opportunities that align with a firm's strategy, saving time and improving the quality of deal flow.
4. **Operational Optimization**
   Within portfolio companies, machine learning can identify inefficiencies, predict customer churn, and optimize supply chains. These insights help private equity firms create value during the ownership period, boosting overall returns.

Success Stories in Machine Learning

The promise of machine learning isn't just theoretical—it's already delivering tangible results. In one case, a private equity firm used machine learning to evaluate a potential acquisition in the retail sector. The algorithm analyzed years of sales data, customer demographics, and market conditions, identifying key drivers of success and potential risks that traditional due diligence had overlooked. Armed with these insights, the firm negotiated a better deal and implemented a more targeted post-acquisition strategy.

In another instance, a private equity firm applied machine learning to streamline the operations of a manufacturing portfolio company. By analyzing procurement and inventory data, the algorithm identified inefficiencies that were costing the company millions annually. The resulting adjustments significantly improved margins and positioned the company for a more lucrative exit.

"These tools are helping us see things we couldn't see before," Griffiths says. "They're not replacing the human element—they're enhancing it."

Challenges in Adoption

Despite its potential, the adoption of machine learning in private equity isn't without obstacles. One of the biggest challenges is data quality. Unlike public markets, where data is standardized and easily accessible, private equity operates in a fragmented landscape. Inconsistent reporting practices and incomplete datasets can make it difficult to train reliable models.

Another hurdle is cultural. Private equity has traditionally been a relationship-driven business, where decisions are often guided by intuition and experience. For some fund managers, the idea of relying on algorithms feels like a departure from the art of investing.

Griffiths acknowledges these concerns but sees them as part of the industry's evolution. "Machine learning doesn't replace human judgment," he explains. "It augments it. The best decisions still come from people—but those decisions are better when they're informed by data."

The Competitive Edge

For firms that embrace these tools, the rewards are significant. Machine learning and big data offer a level of precision and foresight that can provide a critical edge in a highly competitive market. Firms that integrate these technologies into their workflows are better positioned to identify high-potential investments, manage risks, and optimize returns.

"The firms that invest in analytics now are setting themselves up for long-term success," Griffiths says. "It's not just about keeping up—it's about leading the way."

This trend has led to a surge in innovation. Some private equity firms are building in-house data science teams, while others are partnering with technology companies or investing in advanced analytics platforms. The result is a rapidly evolving ecosystem where data and technology are becoming as central to private equity as capital and relationships.

Looking Ahead

The integration of big data and machine learning is still in its early stages, but its impact is already profound. Griffiths envisions a future where advanced analytics are seamlessly embedded in every aspect of private equity, from deal sourcing to portfolio management and exit planning.

"We're just scratching the surface," he says. "The tools we have today are powerful, but they're going to get even better. The challenge is to use them responsibly and intelligently—to leverage their strengths without losing sight of the human element."

For private equity, the implications of this shift are far-reaching. Greater transparency, better decision-making, and more efficient value creation mean the industry is better positioned than ever to deliver on its promise of outsized returns. But the road ahead requires a willingness to adapt—and to embrace the opportunities that technology provides.

"Private equity is changing," Griffiths concludes. "And that's a good thing. These technologies are forcing us to be smarter, more disciplined, and more accountable. They're not just shaping the future of private equity—they're shaping its present."

Leveraging Predictive Analytics for Smarter Investments

Private equity has always been about making informed decisions, but as the industry has grown more complex, the tools and methods for gathering those insights have had to evolve. Predictive analytics, a powerful data-driven approach, is revolutionizing how fund managers identify opportunities, mitigate risks, and maximize returns. Unlike traditional methods, which focus on understanding past performance, predictive analytics anticipates future outcomes, offering private equity firms a clearer view of the road ahead.

This isn't just an incremental improvement; it's a paradigm shift. In an industry where even small missteps can have enormous financial consequences, predictive analytics provides a sharper edge—helping firms allocate capital more wisely, spot risks earlier, and seize opportunities before the competition.

What Predictive Analytics Can Do

Predictive analytics leverages machine learning, statistical modeling, and historical data to uncover patterns that might otherwise go unnoticed. These tools allow private equity firms to anticipate trends, model outcomes, and make decisions with greater confidence. Here are some of its most transformative applications:

1. **Revenue Forecasting**
   Predictive analytics excels at projecting revenue growth for portfolio companies. By analyzing past performance alongside external factors like market conditions and consumer behavior, these tools can provide fund managers with realistic growth scenarios. This insight is invaluable during the due diligence phase, helping firms determine whether a potential investment is worth pursuing.
2. **Identifying Opportunities**
   In a market saturated with options, predictive analytics helps firms focus on the investments with the highest potential. By sifting through vast datasets, these tools can highlight

industries, regions, or companies poised for growth, guiding firms toward opportunities they might otherwise overlook.

3. **Risk Management**
   Predictive models are particularly effective at flagging potential risks. They can identify red flags—such as weakening market positions or operational inefficiencies—long before they escalate into serious problems. This allows fund managers to intervene proactively, protecting their investments.

4. **Optimizing Exit Strategies**
   Predictive analytics also helps determine the optimal timing for exits. By modeling future market conditions, these tools can guide firms on when to sell a portfolio company, ensuring maximum returns while minimizing risks.

Real-World Examples

The impact of predictive analytics isn't theoretical—it's already transforming private equity. Consider a private equity firm evaluating an acquisition in the logistics sector. Using predictive analytics, the firm modeled future demand for the company's services, incorporating variables like fuel prices, shipping trends, and regulatory changes. The analysis revealed strong growth potential in specific regions, enabling the firm to tailor its acquisition strategy and capitalize on those opportunities.

In another case, a private equity firm used predictive analytics to address inefficiencies in a manufacturing portfolio company. By analyzing production data and supply chain metrics, the algorithm identified bottlenecks that were driving up costs. With these insights, the firm implemented targeted changes that reduced expenses by 20%, significantly increasing the company's profitability and overall value.

"These tools are game-changers," says Barry Griffiths, a leader in private equity analytics. "They don't just help us understand what's happening—they help us anticipate what's going to happen. That's the kind of insight that leads to smarter decisions."

Challenges of Implementation

While predictive analytics offers enormous potential, adopting these tools isn't without its hurdles. One major challenge is data quality. Predictive models require clean, comprehensive datasets to produce reliable results. In private equity, where data is often fragmented or inconsistent, this can be a significant barrier.

Another challenge lies in building trust in the technology. Private equity has long been a relationship-driven industry, where intuition and experience hold sway. Convincing fund managers to incorporate predictive analytics into their decision-making processes requires a cultural shift—and a willingness to embrace change.

Griffiths is realistic about these challenges. "No model is perfect," he says. "But the question isn't whether predictive analytics eliminates all uncertainty—it's whether it reduces uncertainty enough to give you an edge. And the answer to that is a resounding yes."

The Competitive Edge

For firms that successfully adopt predictive analytics, the advantages are clear. These tools allow fund managers to make faster, more informed decisions, giving them an edge in a competitive market. They also enable firms to allocate resources more efficiently, ensuring that capital is directed toward the highest-value opportunities.

"Predictive analytics helps us see around corners," Griffiths explains. "It's not about replacing human judgment—it's about enhancing it. The best outcomes come from combining the insights these tools provide with the expertise and instincts our teams bring to the table."

This competitive advantage is driving widespread adoption across the industry. Leading firms are investing heavily in analytics platforms, hiring data scientists, and integrating predictive models into every stage of the investment lifecycle. For these firms, the goal isn't just to keep up—it's to set the pace.

The Future of Predictive Analytics in Private Equity

As predictive analytics technology continues to evolve, its potential applications in private equity will only expand. Griffiths envisions a future where these tools are seamlessly embedded in day-to-day operations, from deal sourcing to portfolio optimization and exit planning.

"We're just scratching the surface," he says. "The tools we have today are powerful, but they're going to get even better. The challenge for us is to use them responsibly, combining their strengths with the human judgment that has always been at the heart of private equity."

For private equity firms, the rise of predictive analytics is both an opportunity and a challenge. Those that embrace these tools will be better positioned to navigate an increasingly complex market and deliver the returns their investors expect. Those that resist risk falling behind.

"The future of private equity isn't just about managing capital," Griffiths concludes. "It's about managing information. And predictive analytics is helping us do that better than ever before."

Overcoming Resistance to Data-Driven Decision Making in Private Equity

Private equity has long been defined by its reliance on relationships, intuition, and experience. Fund managers have built their reputations on the ability to navigate complex deals and identify promising investments, often based on years of accumulated expertise and well-established networks. But as the industry faces increasing complexity, the emergence of data-driven tools is challenging these traditional methods, offering powerful new ways to inform decision-making.

For some firms, these tools represent the future—a competitive advantage that enhances human judgment and unlocks hidden value. For others, they are viewed with skepticism, even resistance. Convincing these firms to embrace data-driven decision-making requires more than technology; it demands a cultural shift, one that preserves the strengths of private equity's legacy while integrating the benefits of modern analytics.

Why Resistance Exists

Resistance to adopting data-driven tools in private equity is rooted in both the industry's history and the practical challenges of change. Several factors contribute to this hesitation:

1. **Cultural Legacy**
   Private equity has always been a relationship-driven business. Deals often emerge from personal connections, and investment decisions are shaped by the instincts of seasoned professionals. Introducing algorithms and predictive models into this equation can feel like a threat to the traditional art of deal-making.

2. **Fear of Disruption**
   Many fund managers worry that data-driven tools will complicate established workflows or shift decision-making away from their control. For firms that have achieved success through traditional methods, the idea of change can be particularly unsettling.
3. **Skepticism of Technology**
   Advanced analytics and machine learning are relatively new to private equity, and their value isn't universally understood. Concerns about the reliability of data and the accuracy of algorithms often fuel skepticism, especially among those unfamiliar with the underlying technology.
4. **Implementation Barriers**
   Adopting data-driven tools requires significant investment in infrastructure, talent, and training. For smaller firms or those with limited resources, these challenges can seem insurmountable, further delaying adoption.

The Case for Change

Despite these obstacles, the case for embracing data-driven decision-making is becoming increasingly clear. In an environment where competition is fierce and investors demand greater accountability, the ability to leverage advanced analytics offers a critical edge.

Barry Griffiths, a leading advocate for analytics in private equity, sees this evolution as a natural progression. "Data-driven tools aren't replacing the human element," he explains. "They're augmenting it. They give us insights we wouldn't have otherwise, helping us make better, faster decisions."

The benefits of data-driven decision-making include:

- **Enhanced Accuracy**: Algorithms can process vast datasets, uncovering patterns and correlations that human analysis might miss. This leads to more accurate assessments of opportunities and risks.
- **Increased Efficiency**: Automating repetitive tasks, like deal screening or financial modeling, frees up fund managers to

focus on high-value activities, such as strategy and negotiation.

- **Improved Transparency**: Advanced analytics provide clear, objective metrics that help build trust with investors, particularly institutional clients who demand detailed reporting and accountability.

Strategies for Overcoming Resistance

Successfully integrating data-driven tools into private equity requires a thoughtful approach that addresses both technical and cultural challenges. Here are some key strategies for driving adoption:

1. **Start Small and Build Trust**
   Rather than overhauling an entire firm's processes, begin with a pilot project. For example, use predictive analytics to evaluate a single deal or optimize one portfolio company's operations. Demonstrating success on a smaller scale can build confidence and generate buy-in.
2. **Show Tangible Results**
   Data-driven tools become far more compelling when their benefits are clear and measurable. Share case studies, metrics, and success stories—both from within the firm and across the industry—to illustrate how these tools lead to better outcomes.
3. **Invest in Education and Training**
   Providing team members with the knowledge and skills to use data-driven tools effectively is critical. Training programs can demystify the technology, helping employees understand how it works and how it complements their expertise.
4. **Position Technology as a Partner**
   Emphasize that advanced analytics are not replacing human judgment but enhancing it. By framing these tools as allies rather than adversaries, firms can alleviate concerns about disruption and loss of control.
5. **Champion Internal Advocates**
   Identify employees who are enthusiastic about analytics and position them as champions within the organization. Their

support and firsthand experience can help persuade others to embrace the change.

6. **Invest in Infrastructure**

   Adoption won't succeed without the right tools and resources. Firms need robust data systems, reliable platforms, and skilled personnel to fully realize the potential of data-driven decision-making.

Lessons from Early Adopters

Some private equity firms have already embraced data-driven decision-making, and their successes provide valuable insights for those considering the transition.

One global firm, for instance, used machine learning algorithms to streamline its deal-sourcing process. By analyzing market data, the algorithms identified high-potential opportunities more efficiently than traditional methods. This not only reduced time spent on due diligence but also allowed the firm to act quickly, gaining a competitive edge.

In another case, a mid-sized firm applied predictive analytics to manage risk across its portfolio. By analyzing operational and market data, the firm identified potential vulnerabilities in two portfolio companies and implemented targeted interventions. These proactive measures preserved value and strengthened investor confidence.

"These examples show that data-driven tools don't replace what we do—they make it better," Griffiths notes. "They help us see around corners, anticipate challenges, and act with precision."

Looking Ahead

As private equity continues to evolve, the integration of data-driven decision-making will become less of an option and more of a necessity. Firms that embrace these tools will be better positioned to navigate market complexities, meet investor expectations, and deliver superior returns.

Griffiths is optimistic about the future but emphasizes that balance is key. "Private equity will always be about people—relationships, judgment, creativity. Those elements will never disappear. But the firms that succeed will be the ones that combine those strengths with the power of data."

The path to adoption won't be without challenges, but for those willing to adapt, the rewards are clear. By overcoming resistance and fostering a culture that values both intuition and innovation, private equity firms can position themselves for long-term success in an increasingly data-driven world.

How Technology is Reshaping Investor Relations

Private equity has always been an industry grounded in trust. Investors commit their capital—often substantial amounts—based on their confidence in a firm's ability to deliver returns. Traditionally, this trust was cultivated through face-to-face meetings, periodic reports, and long-standing relationships. But as the industry has grown more complex and investors have become increasingly sophisticated, these traditional methods are being supplemented, and in some cases replaced, by technology.

Technology is reshaping the way private equity firms interact with investors, enabling more transparency, real-time communication, and tailored reporting. From interactive investor portals to advanced analytics platforms, these tools are not just enhancing communication—they're redefining what investors expect from their private equity partners.

Evolving Investor Expectations

Today's investors, particularly institutional players like pension funds, endowments, and sovereign wealth funds, expect a level of visibility and accountability that wasn't required a decade ago. They're no longer satisfied with quarterly reports and static presentations. Instead, they want detailed performance metrics, real-time updates, and clear insights into how their capital is being managed.

Barry Griffiths, a proponent of technology-driven transparency, views this shift as inevitable. "Investors are more sophisticated now," he explains. "They're asking tougher questions and demanding more robust answers. Technology is how we deliver those answers."

Several factors are driving these heightened expectations:

1. **Increased Competition for Capital**
   With more private equity firms vying for investor dollars, transparency and superior communication have become competitive differentiators.
2. **Regulatory Changes**
   As global regulators push for greater accountability in financial markets, private equity firms face increasing pressure to provide comprehensive disclosures and demonstrate their value.
3. **Influence of Public Market Standards**
   Institutional investors accustomed to the transparency of public markets are now seeking similar levels of visibility from their private equity holdings.

Transformative Tools for Investor Relations

To meet these demands, private equity firms are adopting an array of digital tools designed to enhance the investor experience. Some of the most impactful innovations include:

1. **Interactive Investor Portals**
   Modern investor portals provide centralized platforms where clients can access detailed reports, fund performance dashboards, and real-time updates. These portals often allow investors to customize their views, drilling down into specific funds or portfolio companies.
2. **Advanced Analytics Platforms**
   Performance analytics tools enable firms to present data in an accessible and actionable format. Investors can track cash flows, compare fund performance against benchmarks, and assess risk exposure in real time, empowering them to make more informed decisions.
3. **Automated Reporting Systems**
   Automation has streamlined the preparation and distribution of reports, reducing manual errors and ensuring consistency. These systems allow firms to generate customized reports at scale, saving time while enhancing accuracy.
4. **Real-Time Performance Dashboards**
   Some firms now provide investors with live dashboards that display up-to-date metrics, including portfolio valuations, fund performance, and market conditions. This immediacy helps build trust and keeps investors engaged.
5. **Virtual Engagement Tools**
   From video conferencing to virtual roadshows, digital communication tools are enabling firms to maintain strong relationships with investors, even when in-person meetings aren't possible.

Benefits of Tech-Driven Transparency

The adoption of technology in investor relations isn't just about meeting new demands—it's about building stronger partnerships. By improving communication and transparency, firms can foster greater trust and engagement among their investors. Key benefits include:

- **Enhanced Trust**: Providing investors with real-time access to performance data reassures them that their capital is being managed responsibly and effectively.

- **Stronger Engagement**: Interactive tools and personalized reporting keep investors involved, reinforcing their confidence in the partnership.
- **Operational Efficiency**: Automation reduces the administrative burden on investor relations teams, allowing them to focus on strategic activities.
- **Data-Driven Decisions**: Access to detailed, real-time data helps investors make more informed decisions about their allocations and commitments.

Challenges of Implementation

While the benefits of technology are clear, implementing these tools comes with challenges. The most common obstacles include:

1. **High Costs**
   Building and maintaining sophisticated reporting systems requires significant financial investment, which can be a barrier for smaller firms.
2. **Data Security Concerns**
   Investor portals and real-time systems handle sensitive financial information, making them attractive targets for cyberattacks. Robust cybersecurity measures are essential to protect both the firm and its clients.
3. **Learning Curve**
   Adopting new technology often requires a cultural shift. Both investors and fund managers must adapt to unfamiliar systems and processes, which can be time-consuming and intimidating.

Griffiths acknowledges these challenges but emphasizes that they are surmountable. "The key is to focus on building trust—both in the tools and in the teams using them," he says. "With the right investments in infrastructure and training, the payoff is enormous."

Lessons from Early Adopters

Several private equity firms have already integrated technology into their investor relations strategies, providing valuable lessons for others looking to follow suit.

One global firm launched a cutting-edge investor portal that offered clients real-time access to fund performance and portfolio updates. This transparency not only strengthened relationships but also attracted new investors who were impressed by the firm's commitment to accountability.

Another firm implemented an automated reporting system that dramatically reduced the time required to prepare quarterly updates. By reallocating resources previously spent on manual reporting, the firm was able to focus more on strategic investor engagement, boosting client satisfaction.

"These success stories show what's possible," Griffiths says. "When you use technology to empower investors, it creates a stronger partnership—and that benefits everyone."

The Future of Investor Relations

As technology continues to evolve, its role in investor relations will only grow. Griffiths envisions a future where artificial intelligence and predictive analytics become standard tools for private equity firms, providing investors with deeper insights and forward-looking analyses.

"The next step isn't just showing investors what's happening now," he explains. "It's giving them a view of what's likely to happen next—and how we're positioning their capital for success."

For private equity firms, the message is clear: those that embrace technology will be better equipped to meet investor expectations, build trust, and maintain a competitive edge in an increasingly data-driven world.

"Investor relations is about more than just communication," Griffiths concludes. "It's about creating a partnership based on transparency, trust, and mutual success. Technology helps us do that better than ever before."

The Role of ESG in Shaping Private Equity's Future

Private equity is undergoing a profound transformation. In the past, the industry was primarily concerned with maximizing financial returns, often with little regard for the environmental, social, and governance (ESG) factors that are now reshaping global markets. Today, ESG considerations are no longer a secondary concern— they're becoming a central part of how private equity firms operate, invest, and create value.

What was once viewed as a regulatory burden or a concession to investor demands is now widely recognized as a competitive advantage. Firms that embrace ESG principles are better positioned to navigate risks, seize opportunities, and deliver sustainable returns. The future of private equity, it seems, is as much about responsible investing as it is about profitability.

Why ESG Matters in Private Equity

The rise of ESG in private equity has been driven by a confluence of factors that extend beyond regulatory compliance. These forces are reshaping the way private equity firms think about their responsibilities and their opportunities:

1. **Investor Demands**
   Institutional investors, including pension funds and sovereign wealth funds, are increasingly prioritizing ESG factors in their allocation decisions. Many require detailed disclosures on how firms are managing issues like carbon emissions, labor practices, and governance.
2. **Regulatory Pressures**
   Governments worldwide are introducing stricter ESG-related mandates, from climate reporting requirements to diversity and inclusion guidelines. Compliance is no longer optional— it's a necessity for firms operating in global markets.
3. **Risk Management**
   Ignoring ESG risks can have dire consequences.

Environmental disasters, governance scandals, or labor disputes can tarnish reputations and erode financial performance. ESG principles provide a framework for identifying and mitigating these risks before they materialize.

4. **Value Creation**
    Companies that lead on ESG often outperform their peers in the long term. Private equity firms are increasingly recognizing that sustainable business practices can drive growth, enhance brand reputation, and unlock new market opportunities.

How ESG Is Being Integrated

Private equity firms are weaving ESG considerations into every phase of their operations, from evaluating potential investments to planning exits. Here's how ESG is transforming the investment lifecycle:

1. **Due Diligence**
    ESG assessments are now a critical component of the due diligence process. Firms evaluate potential investments for risks such as unsustainable environmental practices, weak governance structures, or reputational vulnerabilities. This analysis helps ensure that investments align with the firm's ESG standards.

2. **Portfolio Management**
    Post-acquisition, private equity firms work closely with portfolio companies to improve their ESG performance. This might include reducing greenhouse gas emissions, implementing ethical supply chain practices, or enhancing employee diversity. These initiatives not only reduce risk but also position companies for long-term success.

3. **Metrics and Reporting**
    To meet investor and regulatory expectations, firms are adopting standardized ESG metrics. These metrics track progress on sustainability goals and provide transparency to stakeholders, building trust and accountability.

4. **Exit Strategies**
   ESG considerations are increasingly influencing how and when firms exit their investments. Companies with strong ESG credentials tend to attract higher valuations, particularly as buyers prioritize sustainability and governance in their acquisition decisions.

Challenges in ESG Adoption

Despite the clear benefits, integrating ESG principles into private equity isn't without its challenges. The most significant obstacles include:

1. **Inconsistent Standards**
   The lack of universally accepted ESG standards makes it difficult for firms to measure and compare performance. What qualifies as "good" ESG varies widely across regions and industries.
2. **Data Collection**
   Gathering accurate and comprehensive ESG data from portfolio companies can be labor-intensive and complicated. Firms need systems in place to collect, analyze, and report this information effectively.
3. **Short-Term vs. Long-Term Goals**
   Many ESG initiatives require upfront investments that may not yield immediate financial returns. Balancing these costs with the industry's focus on short-term performance metrics can be a challenge.
4. **Skepticism from Stakeholders**
   Some investors and executives remain skeptical of ESG, viewing it as a distraction from financial performance. Overcoming this skepticism requires firms to demonstrate that ESG is not just a moral obligation but also a driver of value.

Technology's Role in ESG Integration

Technology is helping private equity firms overcome these challenges and integrate ESG more effectively. Tools like data analytics, machine learning, and artificial intelligence are proving invaluable for:

- **Identifying Risks**: Algorithms can analyze vast amounts of data to flag ESG risks, such as potential supply chain violations or climate vulnerabilities.
- **Tracking Progress**: Digital platforms allow firms to monitor ESG metrics in real time, providing actionable insights and ensuring accountability.
- **Enhancing Transparency**: Automated reporting tools streamline the process of compiling ESG data, making it easier to meet investor and regulatory requirements.

Barry Griffiths, a strong advocate for ESG integration, sees technology as a catalyst for progress. "With the right tools, we can measure and manage ESG factors with the same rigor as financial performance," he says. "It's about making ESG practical and actionable."

The Competitive Advantage of ESG

Firms that successfully integrate ESG into their operations are gaining a clear edge in the market. By aligning with global trends toward sustainability and inclusivity, they're not only attracting capital but also building more resilient and valuable portfolios.

"ESG isn't just a checkbox exercise," Griffiths emphasizes. "It's a competitive advantage. Firms that lead on ESG will be the ones that attract the best investors, secure the best deals, and build the strongest companies."

Looking Ahead

The integration of ESG into private equity is still a work in progress, but its trajectory is undeniable. As stakeholder expectations continue to evolve, ESG principles will become even more embedded in the fabric of the industry.

Griffiths believes that this shift represents a fundamental redefinition of value. "Private equity has always been about creating value," he says. "What's changing is how we define that value. ESG helps us build companies that aren't just profitable, but also responsible, resilient, and aligned with the world's needs."

For private equity, the rise of ESG is both a challenge and an opportunity. Firms that embrace these principles will not only deliver better returns—they'll help shape a more sustainable and equitable future for everyone.

Private Equity in an Era of Uncertainty and Volatility

Private equity has always thrived on its ability to adapt to complexity and turn challenges into opportunities. But today's landscape—shaped by geopolitical tensions, economic volatility, and rapidly evolving regulatory frameworks—has brought a level of unpredictability that tests even the most seasoned investors. This era of heightened uncertainty is forcing private equity firms to rethink their strategies, adjust their approaches, and innovate like never before.

Despite the challenges, this new environment is fertile ground for firms willing to embrace change. By leveraging advanced tools, refining their investment theses, and doubling down on operational expertise, private equity players can transform volatility into a competitive advantage. Navigating these turbulent waters, however, demands foresight, flexibility, and a willingness to rewrite the rules.

Navigating the Challenges

The challenges private equity firms face today are significant, interconnected, and constantly evolving. Key among them are:

1. **Economic Volatility**
    Rising interest rates, inflationary pressures, and fluctuating global growth forecasts have created a tough backdrop for deal-making. Access to cheap debt—a cornerstone of many private equity strategies—has tightened, forcing firms to rethink how they structure and finance deals. Simultaneously, portfolio companies are under increasing pressure to improve margins and weather economic headwinds.

2. **Geopolitical Instability**
    From supply chain disruptions caused by geopolitical conflicts to trade tensions and energy market upheavals, today's private equity landscape is shaped by forces beyond traditional market dynamics. These risks require firms to assess how global events affect their investments and adapt accordingly.

3. **Regulatory Pressures**
    Governments worldwide are tightening their oversight of private markets. Firms now face increased scrutiny around disclosures, antitrust considerations, and environmental, social, and governance (ESG) factors. This shifting regulatory environment adds layers of complexity to transactions and portfolio management.

4. **Investor Demands**
    Institutional investors are demanding more transparency and accountability than ever before. Beyond financial returns, they now expect regular reporting on ESG performance, risk management strategies, and portfolio resilience.

Each of these challenges forces private equity firms to think beyond traditional playbooks. Barry Griffiths, a seasoned expert in navigating market complexity, sums it up succinctly: "Volatility can be daunting, but it's also where the greatest opportunities lie. Success depends on being prepared, agile, and willing to innovate."

Strategies for Thriving in Uncertain Times

To overcome these challenges and capitalize on opportunities, private equity firms are embracing a range of strategic shifts:

1. **Focus on Diversification**
   Diversification has always been a bedrock of risk management, but in today's environment, it's more critical than ever. Firms are expanding their portfolios across industries, geographies, and asset classes to hedge against localized or sector-specific downturns.
2. **Operational Value Creation**
   With pressure mounting on portfolio companies to deliver results, firms are sharpening their operational expertise. This includes streamlining supply chains, cutting costs, improving efficiency, and finding innovative ways to drive growth.
3. **Flexible Capital Structures**
   The era of cheap debt is over, and private equity firms are adapting by exploring alternative financing options, such as private credit, equity injections, and creative deal structures. This flexibility ensures that deals remain viable even as borrowing costs rise.
4. **Technology as an Enabler**
   Advanced analytics and data-driven decision-making are providing firms with the insights needed to navigate uncertainty. Predictive models, for example, can identify emerging risks, while real-time portfolio dashboards ensure that managers stay informed about market shifts.
5. **Proactive Risk Management**
   Leading firms are investing in more robust risk assessment frameworks. This includes stress testing portfolios, conducting detailed scenario planning, and ensuring that contingency strategies are in place for worst-case scenarios.

Shifting Investment Strategies

Uncertainty is also reshaping how private equity firms approach deal-making. Traditional buyout strategies are evolving, and alternative approaches are gaining traction. Key trends include:

1. **Growth Equity Investments**
   Investing in high-growth companies—particularly in sectors like technology, healthcare, and renewable energy—has become a favored strategy. These companies often need capital to scale, offering strong upside potential for firms willing to take on the associated risks.
2. **Distressed Opportunities**
   Economic volatility creates opportunities to acquire undervalued or distressed assets. Firms with experience in turnarounds are well-positioned to step in, stabilize these businesses, and generate outsized returns.
3. **Infrastructure and Renewables**
   Governments around the world are prioritizing infrastructure and sustainability initiatives. Private equity firms are increasingly drawn to these sectors, seeing them as stable, long-term investment opportunities.
4. **Venture Capital**
   Early-stage investments in cutting-edge fields like artificial intelligence, biotechnology, and clean technology remain attractive for firms with higher risk tolerance. These investments, while speculative, often come with the promise of significant rewards.

The Role of Leadership in Volatility

In uncertain times, strong leadership becomes paramount. Private equity firms must foster a culture of adaptability and empower their teams to respond decisively to changing conditions. This requires:

- **Empowering Teams**: Decentralized decision-making allows teams closer to the ground to act quickly and effectively.
- **Transparent Communication**: Clear, honest communication with stakeholders—including investors, portfolio companies, and employees—builds trust and ensures alignment.
- **Staying Disciplined**: While it's important to adapt, firms must also remain focused on their core strengths and avoid chasing trends without a clear strategic rationale.

Griffiths highlights the importance of resilience. "Uncertainty is a test of leadership. The firms that succeed are those that inspire confidence, act decisively, and stay committed to their values."

Looking Ahead

The challenges facing private equity today are undeniable, but they also represent an inflection point for the industry. Firms that embrace change, adopt new tools, and stay focused on value creation will emerge stronger and more competitive.

"This is a defining moment for private equity," Griffiths observes. "The industry has always thrived on its ability to adapt and innovate. These challenges aren't obstacles—they're opportunities to lead, to create, and to redefine what's possible."

For private equity, the path forward lies in balancing tradition with innovation. By staying true to their principles while embracing new strategies and technologies, firms can turn today's uncertainty into tomorrow's success.

The Growing Influence of Technology-Driven Strategies in Private Equity

Private equity has always thrived on innovation and the ability to adapt to change. In today's environment, technology is redefining the rules of the game. Once considered supplementary, technology-driven strategies have become indispensable, reshaping how deals are sourced, portfolios are managed, and value is created. From artificial intelligence (AI) and machine learning to real-time analytics and automation, private equity is undergoing a transformation fueled by technological advancements.

This shift isn't just about keeping up with competitors; it's about gaining a decisive edge. The firms that integrate technology into their workflows are not only working smarter but also uncovering opportunities and insights that traditional methods often miss. For those willing to embrace these changes, technology is becoming a core driver of success.

Why Technology Is Essential in Private Equity

Private equity operates in a fast-paced and increasingly complex landscape. Deals need to be executed quickly, market conditions shift rapidly, and competition for assets is fierce. Technology offers solutions that address these challenges while unlocking new potential. Its growing importance can be attributed to four key factors:

1. **Speed and Efficiency**
   By automating labor-intensive processes such as financial modeling, due diligence, and portfolio monitoring, technology enables firms to act faster and more decisively.
2. **Enhanced Decision-Making**
   Data analytics tools can process vast amounts of information, revealing patterns and insights that might go unnoticed. These tools allow private equity firms to make more informed decisions with greater confidence.
3. **Risk Mitigation**
   Predictive models and real-time monitoring systems help identify risks early, enabling firms to address potential issues before they escalate.
4. **Competitive Differentiation**
   In a crowded market, the ability to leverage technology to find undervalued assets, optimize operations, and time exits effectively is a significant advantage.

Barry Griffiths, a leader in private equity innovation, puts it succinctly: "Technology isn't a replacement for expertise—it's an amplifier. It allows us to be more precise, more efficient, and ultimately more successful."

Technology in Action: Key Applications

Technology's influence spans the entire investment lifecycle, from deal sourcing to exit strategies. Here's how private equity firms are putting it to work:

1. **Deal Sourcing**
   Traditional deal sourcing often relies on networks and personal relationships, but technology is expanding the playing field. Machine learning algorithms and automated platforms can scan markets, identify high-potential targets, and flag opportunities that align with a firm's strategy. This broadens the scope of potential deals while saving time and resources.
2. **Due Diligence**
   The due diligence process is being revolutionized by advanced analytics. Tools that analyze financial data, industry trends, and operational performance allow firms to evaluate investments faster and more thoroughly. These insights help ensure that no red flags are overlooked.
3. **Portfolio Optimization**
   Once a deal is closed, technology continues to play a vital role. Real-time dashboards and performance monitoring systems provide up-to-date insights into portfolio companies. Predictive analytics can anticipate market shifts, while AI tools help optimize operations, from supply chain efficiency to customer retention strategies.
4. **Exit Planning**
   Technology is transforming how private equity firms plan and execute exits. By analyzing market conditions, buyer behavior, and valuation trends, firms can identify the best time and method for selling a portfolio company, ensuring maximum returns.

Overcoming Barriers to Adoption

While the benefits of technology are clear, integrating it into private equity operations isn't without challenges. Common hurdles include:

1. **Cost of Implementation**
   Advanced tools require substantial investment in infrastructure, software, and skilled personnel. For smaller firms, these costs can be a significant barrier.
2. **Integration Complexity**
   Introducing new technologies into established workflows can disrupt operations. Ensuring seamless integration with existing processes is critical for minimizing disruption.
3. **Resistance to Change**
   The private equity industry has traditionally been relationship-driven, and some professionals are hesitant to rely on data-driven methods. Building trust in technology's capabilities requires education and evidence of its effectiveness.
4. **Data Security**
   As firms handle increasingly sensitive data, robust cybersecurity measures are essential to protect both internal operations and investor trust.

Griffiths acknowledges these challenges but emphasizes their solvability. "The barriers to technology adoption are real, but they're not insurmountable," he says. "With the right strategy and commitment, any firm can unlock the value that technology offers."

Success Stories: Real-World Impact

Private equity firms that have embraced technology are already reaping the rewards. For example:

- **Enhanced Deal Sourcing**: A mid-sized firm implemented an AI-driven platform that identified a lucrative investment in an overlooked market segment. This deal would have likely gone unnoticed using traditional sourcing methods.
- **Operational Efficiency**: A large private equity firm used machine learning to analyze data from a struggling portfolio company. The insights revealed inefficiencies in the supply chain, leading to changes that boosted margins by 15%.
- **Strategic Exits**: Using predictive analytics, another firm forecasted market demand for a portfolio company's

products, enabling a strategically timed exit that exceeded valuation expectations.

"These aren't isolated cases," Griffiths notes. "They're proof of what's possible when you combine expertise with the right technology."

The Future of Technology in Private Equity

The role of technology in private equity is poised to grow even further. Emerging tools such as blockchain, advanced AI, and enhanced data visualization are set to revolutionize the industry in ways we are only beginning to understand.

Griffiths envisions a future where technology is fully integrated into every aspect of private equity. "Firms that lead the way on technology adoption won't just survive—they'll define the future of this industry," he says. "But it's not just about having the tools. It's about using them intelligently, in combination with the judgment and creativity that private equity has always relied on."

Balancing Innovation with Expertise

While technology offers immense potential, it's important to strike a balance. The tools are only as effective as the people using them. Firms must continue to prioritize the human elements that have always driven success—intuition, relationships, and strategic vision.

Griffiths emphasizes this point. "Technology is a means to an end, not the end itself. The best firms will be those that integrate it seamlessly, using it to enhance—not replace—their core strengths."

A New Era for Private Equity

Technology is reshaping private equity in profound ways, offering tools that make firms faster, smarter, and more competitive. But this transformation isn't just about adopting the latest innovations—it's about rethinking how value is created in a dynamic and data-driven world.

As the industry continues to evolve, private equity firms must embrace technology not as an optional upgrade, but as an essential part of their strategy. Those that do will be well-positioned to navigate the complexities of today's markets and lead the industry into the future.

The Evolution of Private Equity in Emerging Markets

Emerging markets have long captured the imagination of private equity investors. These regions, with their promise of rapid economic growth and untapped opportunities, offer the allure of high returns. Yet they also come with inherent challenges—political volatility, regulatory hurdles, and economic unpredictability. Despite these risks, the narrative around emerging markets has shifted significantly in recent years. No longer viewed solely as volatile frontiers, these regions are increasingly seen as engines of global growth, driven by innovation, urbanization, and the rise of a powerful middle class.

For private equity firms, this evolution presents a unique opportunity. It's no longer just about chasing growth; it's about actively shaping it. By employing refined strategies, partnering with local experts, and committing to long-term investments, firms are transforming emerging markets into vital components of their global portfolios.

Why Emerging Markets Matter

The growing importance of emerging markets is undeniable. These regions, which now contribute significantly to global GDP growth, offer distinct advantages for private equity investors:

1. **Rapid Economic Growth**
   Many emerging markets, such as those in Southeast Asia, Sub-Saharan Africa, and parts of Latin America, are experiencing GDP growth rates that far outpace those of developed economies. Key sectors like technology, healthcare, and infrastructure are expanding rapidly, offering fertile ground for investment.
2. **Demographic Advantage**
   Emerging markets are home to young, dynamic populations that drive demand for consumer goods, digital services, and infrastructure. In countries like India and Indonesia, the rise

of a middle class is reshaping economies and creating new opportunities for private equity.

3. **Untapped Potential**
Unlike developed markets, where industries are often saturated, many sectors in emerging markets remain fragmented or underserved. This allows private equity firms to step in, consolidate market players, and build industry leaders.

4. **Infrastructure Development**
Governments across emerging markets are heavily investing in infrastructure to support economic growth. These initiatives open doors for private equity investments in transportation, energy, and telecommunications.

Challenges in Emerging Markets

While the potential of emerging markets is immense, they come with a unique set of challenges that demand careful navigation:

1. **Regulatory Uncertainty**
Inconsistent regulations, bureaucratic inefficiencies, and shifting government policies can create obstacles for private equity deals and portfolio management.

2. **Currency Risk**
Fluctuations in local currencies can significantly impact returns, particularly for firms relying on hard currency valuations.

3. **Political Instability**
Geopolitical tensions and domestic unrest can create unpredictable conditions, affecting both portfolio companies and the broader investment climate.

4. **Data and Transparency Issues**
Access to reliable financial data and consistent reporting standards is often limited, complicating due diligence and portfolio oversight.

Barry Griffiths, a seasoned investor in emerging markets, emphasizes the importance of preparation. "You have to understand the market inside out," he says. "Building local relationships, understanding the cultural and regulatory nuances, and taking a long-term view are critical to success."

Strategies for Success

Private equity firms are finding innovative ways to manage risks and unlock value in emerging markets. The most successful strategies include:

1. **Partnering with Local Experts**
   Building alliances with local investors, operators, and advisors provides valuable insights into market dynamics and regulatory frameworks. These partnerships are often the key to navigating complex environments effectively.
2. **Sector Specialization**
   Firms that focus on sectors where they have deep expertise—such as technology, healthcare, or renewable energy—are better equipped to manage risks and identify opportunities.
3. **Adopting a Long-Term Perspective**
   Emerging markets often require patience. Investments in these regions may take longer to mature, but a long-term commitment allows firms to capitalize on sustainable growth.
4. **Mitigating Risks**
   Tools like currency hedging, diversified investment portfolios, and rigorous due diligence processes are essential for managing the risks inherent in emerging markets.
5. **Integrating ESG Principles**
   Environmental, social, and governance (ESG) considerations are especially critical in emerging markets, where issues like sustainability and labor practices can significantly impact value creation. Firms that prioritize ESG often see stronger performance and reduced risks.

Emerging Markets in Focus

Several regions stand out as hotspots for private equity investment:

- **Southeast Asia**: With its youthful populations and rapid digital adoption, Southeast Asia offers opportunities in e-commerce, fintech, and renewable energy.
- **Sub-Saharan Africa**: Natural resource wealth and expanding consumer markets make Africa attractive for investments in agriculture, energy, and financial services.
- **Latin America**: Countries like Brazil, Mexico, and Colombia are seeing growth in healthcare, technology, and consumer goods, supported by an expanding middle class.
- **Middle East and North Africa (MENA)**: Economic diversification efforts, particularly in the Gulf states, are creating opportunities in logistics, infrastructure, and clean energy.

Success Stories

Several private equity firms have demonstrated the potential of emerging markets through successful investments:

- **Consumer Goods in India**: A private equity firm invested in a mid-sized consumer goods company, leveraging local expertise to improve distribution and expand into rural markets. After six years, the firm exited with a 3.5x return.
- **Renewable Energy in Africa**: A private equity fund supported the development of solar power projects in Sub-Saharan Africa, providing clean energy to underserved communities. The project delivered strong financial returns while meeting critical social and environmental needs.
- **Technology in Southeast Asia**: By backing a fintech startup in Indonesia, a private equity firm helped the company scale to millions of users, eventually leading to a successful IPO.

"These stories highlight the potential of emerging markets," Griffiths explains. "The returns are there, but they require a combination of vision, patience, and execution."

Looking Ahead

Emerging markets are poised to play an increasingly pivotal role in the global private equity landscape. As these regions continue to drive economic growth and innovation, they present unparalleled opportunities for firms willing to navigate their complexities.

Griffiths sees the rise of emerging markets as a defining moment for private equity. "The potential here is enormous," he says. "But it's not just about following the growth—it's about leading it. Firms that understand how to build value in these markets will shape the future of the industry."

For private equity, the message is clear: emerging markets are no longer a side story—they are central to the narrative of global investment. By approaching these regions with diligence, adaptability, and a long-term perspective, firms can unlock transformative opportunities and help shape the next chapter of global economic progress.

Private Equity's Role in the Global Energy Transition

The global energy landscape is shifting at an unprecedented pace. As nations grapple with the urgent challenge of combating climate change, the transition from fossil fuels to renewable energy has become both a moral imperative and an economic opportunity. Governments, corporations, and investors are funneling trillions of dollars into clean energy initiatives, and private equity is emerging as a key player in this transformative era.

For private equity firms, the energy transition isn't just a chance to align with ESG principles—it's an opportunity to invest in the infrastructure and technology that will define the future. By backing renewable energy projects, supporting groundbreaking technologies, and helping portfolio companies adopt sustainable practices, private equity can accelerate this transition while generating robust returns.

Why the Energy Transition Is Critical

The energy transition is being driven by a combination of economic, political, and social forces that are reshaping global priorities:

1. **Regulatory Push**
   Governments around the world are enacting aggressive policies to cut carbon emissions and promote renewable

energy. Programs like the European Green Deal and the U.S. Inflation Reduction Act provide financial incentives and regulatory clarity, creating a fertile environment for clean energy investments.

2. **Cost Competitiveness**
   Renewable energy sources like solar and wind have become increasingly cost-effective, rivaling or even surpassing fossil fuels in affordability. Advances in energy storage technologies are further enhancing the economic case for renewables.

3. **Investor and Consumer Demand**
   Institutional investors are prioritizing ESG performance, pushing private equity firms to adopt sustainability strategies. Simultaneously, consumers are demanding greener products and services, forcing companies to adapt or risk losing market share.

4. **Climate Crisis Response**
   The urgency of the climate crisis has catalyzed a global shift in energy priorities. Businesses and governments alike are recognizing the need for bold action to decarbonize the economy and limit global warming.

How Private Equity Is Driving the Transition

Private equity is uniquely positioned to facilitate the energy transition. With access to significant capital and a mandate to drive operational improvements, private equity firms can play a transformative role in the clean energy revolution. Key areas of impact include:

1. **Investing in Renewable Energy**
   Many private equity firms are pouring capital into renewable energy projects such as wind farms, solar installations, and hydropower plants. These assets offer long-term, stable returns and align with the growing demand for clean energy.

2. **Improving Energy Efficiency**
   Private equity-backed companies are increasingly adopting

energy-efficient technologies to reduce operational costs and lower carbon footprints. These measures range from upgrading equipment to retrofitting buildings with modern, energy-saving systems.
3. **Funding Innovative Technologies**
Emerging technologies like hydrogen energy, advanced battery storage, and carbon capture are essential for achieving net-zero emissions. Private equity firms are providing the capital needed to develop and scale these innovations.
4. **Repurposing Fossil Fuel Assets**
Some firms are acquiring traditional energy assets with the goal of transitioning them toward renewable operations. By managing these transitions responsibly, private equity can reduce emissions while maintaining energy reliability.

Challenges in the Energy Transition

Despite the opportunities, the energy transition presents unique challenges that private equity firms must navigate:

1. **High Upfront Costs**
Renewable energy projects and clean technology development often require significant initial investments. Smaller firms may struggle to allocate the necessary capital without straining resources.
2. **Regulatory Complexity**
The energy sector operates under a patchwork of regulations that vary widely across regions and jurisdictions. Understanding and complying with these rules is essential to avoid legal and operational risks.
3. **Market Volatility**
Energy markets are highly sensitive to geopolitical events, commodity price fluctuations, and technological advancements. Managing this volatility requires careful risk assessment and contingency planning.
4. **Unproven Technologies**
Investing in emerging technologies comes with uncertainty about scalability, adoption rates, and long-term viability.

Firms must strike a balance between taking calculated risks and ensuring returns.

Barry Griffiths, a seasoned private equity investor with experience in clean energy projects, acknowledges these obstacles. "The challenges are real, but they're manageable," he explains. "What's needed is a disciplined approach that combines financial expertise with a deep understanding of the energy landscape."

Success Stories from the Energy Transition

Several private equity firms have already demonstrated the potential for strong returns while driving meaningful impact:

- **Wind Energy Projects**: A leading private equity firm financed the development of offshore wind farms in Europe, providing clean electricity to millions of households. The initiative not only delivered strong financial returns but also contributed significantly to regional climate goals.
- **Battery Storage Breakthroughs**: Another firm backed a startup specializing in advanced energy storage technologies. With private equity support, the company scaled its operations and secured major contracts with renewable energy providers.
- **Efficiency Overhauls**: A mid-sized private equity firm worked with its portfolio companies to implement energy-saving measures, such as installing energy-efficient HVAC systems and transitioning to LED lighting. These changes reduced costs and improved ESG scores across the portfolio.

"These are more than investment successes," Griffiths points out. "They're proof that private equity can be a force for good, driving the solutions we need to address climate change."

The Path Forward: Private Equity's Role in Clean Energy

The energy transition is still in its early stages, and private equity will play a critical role in shaping its trajectory. Griffiths envisions private equity firms acting as catalysts for innovation, scaling new technologies, and transforming industries to meet the demands of a decarbonized future.

"The energy transition isn't just an investment opportunity—it's a responsibility," he says. "Private equity has the resources, expertise, and influence to accelerate this shift. But it requires vision and a commitment to long-term value creation."

Looking ahead, private equity's involvement in the energy transition is likely to expand, encompassing not only renewable energy projects but also adjacent sectors like sustainable agriculture, electric mobility, and green infrastructure. Firms that align their strategies with these trends will be well-positioned to lead in a low-carbon economy.

Balancing Profit and Purpose

One of the defining challenges for private equity in the energy transition is striking the right balance between financial returns and social responsibility. Griffiths argues that the two goals are increasingly aligned. "Sustainability and profitability go hand in hand," he explains. "The companies that lead on ESG will not only perform better but also create lasting value for all stakeholders."

A Generational Opportunity

The global energy transition represents one of the greatest investment opportunities of our time. For private equity, it's a chance to drive meaningful change, deliver exceptional returns, and help shape a sustainable future. By embracing this challenge, the industry can redefine its role in the economy and leave a lasting legacy.

"The energy transition is happening now," Griffiths concludes. "The question is, will we lead the way or fall behind? Private equity has the tools to make a difference—now it's up to us to use them."

The Impact of Geopolitics on Private Equity Strategy

The influence of geopolitics on private equity has never been more profound. From trade tensions to regulatory upheavals and regional conflicts, the global political landscape increasingly shapes the environment in which private equity firms operate. These forces affect every stage of the investment lifecycle, creating both risks and opportunities. For firms prepared to navigate this complexity, geopolitics can serve as a source of strategic advantage rather than a roadblock.

As globalization evolves into a more fragmented paradigm, the interconnected nature of economies means that no region or sector operates in isolation. This reality underscores the need for private equity firms to anticipate geopolitical shifts, adapt their strategies, and build resilience into their portfolios.

Geopolitical Forces Reshaping Private Equity

Several key geopolitical trends are defining the private equity landscape today:

1. **Regional Instability and Conflicts**
   Conflicts in regions like Eastern Europe, the Middle East, and Southeast Asia create ripple effects far beyond their borders. Disruptions to supply chains, energy markets, and capital flows can destabilize entire industries, requiring firms to pivot quickly.
2. **Trade Wars and Protectionism**
   The rise of protectionist policies and trade disputes, particularly between major economies like the United States and China, has complicated cross-border investment strategies. Tariffs, export controls, and shifting trade agreements can alter the cost structures and market opportunities for portfolio companies.
3. **Energy and Resource Competition**
   Access to critical resources like rare earth minerals, essential for renewable energy and advanced technology, has become a geopolitical flashpoint. This competition is reshaping energy markets and influencing private equity strategies in related sectors.
4. **Regulatory Divergence**
   Governments are adopting increasingly varied approaches to regulation, particularly in areas such as data privacy, antitrust, and ESG compliance. This divergence requires firms to navigate a patchwork of rules that can significantly impact deal execution and portfolio management.
5. **Supply Chain Realignments**
   Geopolitical events, such as the COVID-19 pandemic and rising tensions between major trading partners, have exposed vulnerabilities in global supply chains. Firms are now prioritizing diversification and regionalization to reduce dependence on any single market.

How Geopolitics Impacts Private Equity Strategy

The effects of geopolitics are felt across every phase of private equity investment. Understanding these impacts is critical to maintaining agility and competitiveness:

1. **Deal Sourcing and Evaluation**
   Geopolitical considerations now play a central role in deal sourcing. Firms must assess not only the financial health of potential targets but also their exposure to political risks such as sanctions, regulatory changes, or supply chain vulnerabilities.
2. **Valuations and Pricing**
   Geopolitical uncertainty can lead to fluctuating valuations as markets reassess risk. While this creates challenges, it also presents opportunities to acquire undervalued assets in regions or industries temporarily affected by instability.
3. **Portfolio Diversification**
   To mitigate risk, many firms are adopting more diversified strategies, spreading investments across regions and sectors to reduce exposure to specific geopolitical pressures.
4. **Exit Timing and Execution**
   Geopolitical factors often dictate the timing and structure of exits. Currency volatility, regulatory hurdles, or shifting market sentiment can lead firms to delay exits or pursue alternative strategies, such as selling to local buyers.

Barry Griffiths, a private equity veteran, emphasizes the importance of integrating geopolitical analysis into strategic planning. "Geopolitics isn't just background noise—it's a critical factor that shapes the opportunities and risks we face," he says. "The firms that thrive are those that incorporate it into every decision."

Strategies for Navigating Geopolitical Uncertainty

To successfully navigate the complexities of geopolitics, private equity firms are adopting forward-looking strategies designed to enhance resilience and adaptability:

1. **Scenario Planning**
   By modeling potential outcomes of geopolitical events—such as changes in trade policy or regional conflicts—firms can identify vulnerabilities in their portfolios and prepare contingency plans.
2. **Local Expertise and Partnerships**
   Building strong relationships with local advisors, operators, and investors helps firms navigate regulatory nuances and cultural dynamics. These partnerships are invaluable for understanding on-the-ground realities.
3. **Enhanced Risk Management**
   Firms are integrating geopolitical risk assessments into their broader risk management frameworks. This includes conducting stress tests, monitoring political developments, and evaluating exposure to key markets.
4. **Investing in Resilient Sectors**
   Certain industries, such as healthcare, technology, and renewable energy, are less susceptible to geopolitical disruptions. Targeting these sectors can help firms build portfolios that are better positioned to weather instability.
5. **Advocacy and Engagement**
   Active engagement with policymakers and industry groups allows firms to advocate for favorable regulatory environments and stay informed about policy changes that could affect their investments.

Case Studies: Adapting to Geopolitical Realities

Successful navigation of geopolitical challenges requires a combination of foresight and flexibility. The following examples illustrate how private equity firms have adapted to geopolitical shifts:

- **Supply Chain Diversification**: In response to trade tensions between the U.S. and China, a private equity firm restructured the supply chain of a portfolio company in the consumer goods sector. By establishing alternative production facilities in Southeast Asia, the firm reduced exposure to tariffs and minimized disruptions.

- **Navigating Sanctions**: A firm operating in a region affected by international sanctions worked closely with legal and compliance experts to ensure operations remained within regulatory guidelines. The firm also sought alternative markets, preserving profitability despite geopolitical challenges.
- **Capitalizing on Energy Trends**: Another firm leveraged geopolitical support for renewable energy initiatives to invest in wind and solar projects in Europe. These investments not only delivered strong returns but also aligned with broader decarbonization goals.

"These examples highlight the importance of agility," Griffiths observes. "It's about recognizing risks early and turning them into opportunities."

The Future of Geopolitics in Private Equity

As global political and economic landscapes continue to evolve, geopolitics will remain a central consideration for private equity firms. Griffiths believes that success in this environment will require a mindset of constant vigilance and adaptability. "The pace of change is accelerating," he says. "Firms need to be proactive, not reactive, when it comes to geopolitical risks."

For private equity, geopolitics is not just a challenge—it's an opportunity to build more resilient, diversified, and innovative portfolios. By integrating geopolitical considerations into every aspect of their strategy, firms can position themselves for long-term success in an increasingly complex world.

Redefining Private Equity's Role in Economic Development

Private equity has long been a catalyst for economic growth, helping companies scale, fostering innovation, and creating jobs. But as the global economy evolves, so too does the role of private equity. Today, the industry is increasingly called upon to address broader societal challenges such as inequality, sustainability, and resilience in underserved markets. For private equity firms, this shift represents not only a responsibility but also an opportunity to align long-term financial success with meaningful economic development.

By prioritizing investments that create shared value, private equity firms can enhance their reputations, attract mission-driven investors, and contribute to sustainable growth. This new era of private equity isn't just about profits—it's about building an enduring legacy.

The Economic Impact of Private Equity

Private equity's role in driving economic development is multidimensional, with measurable impacts across various sectors and communities:

1. **Job Creation**
   Private equity-backed companies often experience significant growth, leading to increased hiring. From entry-level positions to executive roles, this expansion fuels local economies and creates opportunities for individuals.
2. **Innovation and Competitiveness**
   Through targeted investments, private equity firms enable companies to develop new technologies, improve processes, and compete on a global stage. This innovation drives economic dynamism and enhances industries.
3. **Access to Capital**
   Private equity provides vital funding to businesses that might struggle to secure financing through traditional means. This is especially true for small and medium-sized enterprises (SMEs) and businesses in emerging markets.

4. **Infrastructure Development**
   Investments in physical and digital infrastructure—such as transportation systems, renewable energy, and broadband networks—lay the groundwork for broader economic growth and social advancement.
5. **Economic Resilience**
   By improving operational efficiency and scalability, private equity helps portfolio companies weather economic challenges, ensuring their long-term viability and contribution to local economies.

Evolving Expectations of Private Equity

As the influence of private equity has grown, so too have expectations from stakeholders, including institutional investors, policymakers, and the public. Firms are now being asked to play a more active role in addressing societal challenges:

1. **Sustainability Leadership**
   Environmental, social, and governance (ESG) considerations are no longer optional. Investors expect private equity firms to prioritize sustainability, reduce carbon footprints, and champion responsible business practices.
2. **Inclusive Growth**
   Economic development must benefit all segments of society. Firms are increasingly held accountable for ensuring their investments promote diversity, equity, and inclusion.
3. **Local Economic Impact**
   Firms are being challenged to invest in ways that strengthen local supply chains, create regional hubs of innovation, and generate value that stays within communities.
4. **Transparency and Accountability**
   As stakeholders demand greater insight into the social and economic outcomes of private equity investments, firms must adopt robust reporting practices to demonstrate their impact.

Strategies for Aligning Private Equity with Economic Development

To redefine their role, private equity firms are adopting strategies that balance financial returns with broader societal benefits:

1. **Impact Investing**
   Impact investments target measurable social or environmental outcomes alongside financial performance. Sectors like renewable energy, healthcare, and affordable housing are particularly ripe for impact-driven strategies.
2. **Public-Private Partnerships**
   Collaborations with governments and non-governmental organizations (NGOs) enable private equity firms to amplify their investments. These partnerships can unlock funding, reduce risks, and ensure projects address systemic challenges.
3. **Supporting SMEs and Entrepreneurs**
   Private equity firms are increasingly focusing on nurturing small and medium-sized enterprises, which are critical to job creation and economic resilience. Providing capital and operational expertise helps these businesses grow sustainably.
4. **Workforce Development**
   By investing in workforce training and education, firms can enhance employee skills, drive productivity, and ensure long-term competitiveness for their portfolio companies.
5. **ESG Integration**
   Firms are embedding ESG metrics into their decision-making processes, tracking everything from carbon emissions to community impact. This data not only demonstrates accountability but also informs strategies for continuous improvement.

Case Studies: Private Equity Driving Economic Development

Firms that have embraced economic development as a core part of their mission offer compelling examples of what's possible:

- **Revitalizing Local Economies**: A private equity firm partnered with local authorities to reinvigorate a declining industrial region. By modernizing manufacturing facilities, implementing sustainable practices, and creating high-paying jobs, the firm drove economic revitalization while achieving strong returns.

- **Improving Access to Healthcare**: Another firm invested in a network of rural healthcare providers, expanding services to underserved areas. The initiative not only improved health outcomes but also established a scalable business model that delivered consistent profits.
- **Expanding Renewable Energy Access**: A firm specializing in infrastructure investments funded solar power projects in remote regions. The projects provided clean, affordable energy to communities, enabling economic activity while contributing to global decarbonization goals.

"These stories show the power of private equity when it's aligned with the needs of society," says Barry Griffiths, an advocate for sustainable investing. "It's about creating value that extends beyond financial metrics."

Challenges to Aligning Private Equity with Economic Development

While the benefits are clear, pursuing economic development goals comes with challenges:

1. **Balancing Returns and Impact**
   Meeting investor expectations for high returns while achieving measurable societal impact requires careful planning and execution. Firms must ensure that these goals complement rather than compete with one another.
2. **Navigating Regulatory Environments**
   Economic development initiatives often involve complex regulatory landscapes, particularly in emerging markets. Building local expertise is essential for overcoming these hurdles.
3. **Impact Measurement**
   Quantifying social and economic impact remains an evolving practice. Standardized metrics and transparent reporting are

critical to demonstrating success and maintaining stakeholder confidence.

4. **Stakeholder Alignment**
Balancing the priorities of diverse stakeholders—including investors, governments, and communities—requires effective communication and collaboration.

Looking Ahead: A Broader Mandate for Private Equity

As the global economy faces challenges ranging from climate change to inequality, private equity is uniquely positioned to be a force for good. By aligning investment strategies with the principles of economic development, firms can drive transformative change while securing sustainable growth.

Griffiths envisions a future where private equity firms are leaders in addressing global challenges. "The industry has the capital, expertise, and reach to tackle the world's biggest problems," he says. "But it takes vision and a commitment to thinking beyond short-term gains."

For private equity, the mandate is clear: embrace a broader role in fostering sustainable, inclusive growth. Firms that rise to this challenge will not only create value for their investors but also leave a lasting positive impact on the world.

Building a Legacy

Private equity is at a crossroads. The industry's ability to drive economic development represents an opportunity to redefine its legacy and prove that financial success and societal impact are not mutually exclusive. By committing to investments that create lasting value for all stakeholders, private equity can build a future where profit and progress go hand in hand.

As Griffiths concludes, "This is our moment to lead. Private equity has always been about unlocking potential—now it's time to unlock potential not just for companies, but for communities and economies as well."

Preparing for the Next Decade in Private Equity

Private equity stands at the threshold of a new era. The next decade will be shaped by a convergence of global challenges—climate change, geopolitical instability, technological disruption, and shifting societal expectations. For private equity firms, these challenges are not just hurdles to overcome; they are opportunities to lead, innovate, and redefine their role in the global economy.

The firms that succeed will be those that anticipate change, adapt swiftly, and embrace a vision that extends beyond immediate financial returns. By aligning their strategies with the evolving demands of stakeholders and harnessing emerging trends, private equity can position itself as a transformative force in business and society.

The Forces Shaping the Future

Several key forces will define the next decade for private equity, reshaping how firms operate and create value:

1. **Sustainability and ESG Imperatives**
   Environmental, social, and governance (ESG) considerations are no longer optional—they are fundamental. Investors,

regulators, and consumers are demanding greater accountability, transparency, and action on sustainability issues. Firms that integrate ESG into their strategies will build stronger portfolios and long-term resilience.

2. **Technological Evolution**
   The rise of artificial intelligence, machine learning, blockchain, and automation is transforming industries. These technologies offer new investment opportunities and tools to enhance operational efficiency and decision-making.

3. **The Energy Transition**
   As the world shifts from fossil fuels to renewable energy, private equity has a critical role to play in funding clean energy projects, advancing sustainable technologies, and supporting the decarbonization of traditional industries.

4. **Geopolitical Instability**
   Trade disputes, regional conflicts, and regulatory divergence will continue to disrupt markets. Firms must develop strategies to navigate these complexities, from diversifying investments to mitigating supply chain risks.

5. **Evolving Investor Expectations**
   Institutional investors increasingly prioritize impact, transparency, and measurable outcomes. Private equity firms must enhance their reporting capabilities and demonstrate alignment with these values.

6. **Emerging Markets and Demographic Shifts**
   Population growth and urbanization in emerging markets will drive demand for infrastructure, healthcare, technology, and consumer goods. Firms that establish a presence in these regions will unlock significant growth potential.

Strategic Imperatives for Success

To thrive in this rapidly evolving landscape, private equity firms must adopt strategies that emphasize adaptability, innovation, and collaboration:

1. **Prioritize Value Creation**
   Value creation now extends beyond financial engineering. Firms must focus on improving operational performance,

scaling portfolio companies, and fostering innovation to drive sustainable growth.

2. **Harness the Power of Data and Analytics**
   Advanced analytics, artificial intelligence, and machine learning can uncover hidden opportunities, identify risks, and streamline decision-making. Firms that invest in these tools will gain a decisive edge.

3. **Build Resilient Portfolios**
   Diversification across sectors, geographies, and asset classes is essential to mitigate risk. Firms should also stress-test portfolios to prepare for economic shocks, geopolitical events, and market disruptions.

4. **Deepen ESG Integration**
   Incorporating ESG metrics into every stage of the investment lifecycle—from due diligence to exit planning—will not only enhance impact but also attract investors and strengthen long-term returns.

5. **Expand into High-Growth Markets**
   Establishing local partnerships and building expertise in emerging markets will position firms to capitalize on opportunities in regions experiencing rapid economic and demographic change.

6. **Enhance Stakeholder Engagement**
   Transparent, consistent communication with investors, regulators, and communities will build trust and ensure alignment with broader societal goals. Robust reporting on both financial and non-financial performance will become a competitive differentiator.

Lessons from Industry Leaders

Barry Griffiths, a seasoned private equity professional, emphasizes the importance of staying ahead of trends. "The pace of change is accelerating," he says. "The firms that thrive in the next decade will be those that anticipate disruptions and position themselves proactively."

Griffiths points to key lessons from firms that have successfully adapted to change:

- **Adaptability in Crisis**: During the COVID-19 pandemic, a firm restructured its portfolio to prioritize digital-first businesses and supply chain resilience. This foresight enabled the firm to outperform peers and capitalize on emerging opportunities.
- **Investing in Innovation**: A leading private equity firm launched a dedicated fund for emerging technologies, targeting AI, biotech, and cleantech. By aligning with high-growth sectors, the firm achieved outsized returns while supporting transformative solutions.
- **Driving ESG Leadership**: Another firm embedded ESG principles into its investment framework, achieving measurable outcomes such as carbon neutrality and workforce diversity across its portfolio. These efforts strengthened its reputation and attracted impact-focused investors.

"These examples show that success isn't about reacting—it's about anticipating," Griffiths observes. "Proactive firms will lead the way."

Opportunities for Innovation and Growth

The coming decade presents immense opportunities for firms willing to innovate and expand their horizons. Key areas of focus include:

1. **Digital Transformation**
   The shift to digital economies continues to accelerate. Investments in digital infrastructure, e-commerce platforms, and fintech solutions will be critical for capturing growth.
2. **Healthcare and Life Sciences**
   Advances in biotechnology, personalized medicine, and healthcare delivery are creating opportunities to invest in sectors that address critical societal needs while delivering robust returns.
3. **Sustainable Infrastructure**
   As governments and businesses prioritize green infrastructure, private equity firms can play a central role in

funding renewable energy projects, public transportation systems, and smart cities.
4. **Education and Workforce Development**
Investments in education technology and workforce training will address the skills gap created by automation, enabling both economic development and strong returns.

Redefining Private Equity

The next decade will demand bold action and a redefined vision of private equity's role in the global economy. Firms must go beyond traditional approaches, embracing innovation, collaboration, and a commitment to creating shared value.

"This is a transformative moment for private equity," Griffiths concludes. "We have the tools, the capital, and the expertise to drive change—not just for our investors but for the world. It's time to step up and lead."

The private equity industry is poised to shape the future of business, technology, and society. By preparing for what's ahead and committing to a long-term perspective, firms can ensure their success while contributing to a more resilient and equitable global economy.

Private Equity's Role in Shaping the Future

Private equity is standing on the threshold of transformation. The industry faces an inflection point where challenges such as climate change, technological disruption, and geopolitical uncertainty intersect with unparalleled opportunities for growth, innovation, and impact. The next decade will demand more than strategic agility; it will require a redefinition of the industry's purpose and approach.

The private equity firms that thrive in this environment will not only deliver robust financial returns but will also play a pivotal role in shaping a better global economy. This shift goes beyond adaptation—it is about leadership, innovation, and responsibility.

The Imperatives for Success

As the private equity landscape evolves, five central imperatives will guide the industry's path forward:

1. **Sustainability as Strategy**
    Sustainability has moved from a niche consideration to a core strategic pillar. Firms that embed environmental, social, and governance (ESG) principles into their investment processes will build more resilient portfolios, attract mission-aligned capital, and meet the growing demands of stakeholders.
2. **Technology as a Catalyst**
    Technology is revolutionizing how private equity operates. From AI-powered analytics to blockchain-enabled transparency, firms must leverage cutting-edge tools to enhance efficiency, uncover new opportunities, and drive innovation across their investments.
3. **Global Growth with Purpose**
    The rise of emerging markets, urbanization, and demographic shifts offers immense potential for private equity. By engaging thoughtfully in these regions, firms can foster inclusive growth while tapping into expanding consumer and infrastructure demands.
4. **Accountability and Transparency**
    Stakeholders now expect more than financial results—they demand clarity and accountability. Firms that prioritize transparent reporting, engage with communities, and measure impact will build trust and differentiate themselves in a competitive market.
5. **Balancing Profit with Purpose**
    The private equity industry has the unique ability to achieve strong returns while addressing critical global challenges. Firms that balance financial performance with meaningful societal contributions will emerge as leaders in the new era of investing.

A Vision for the Future

Barry Griffiths, a veteran in the private equity space, articulates the opportunity with clarity: "Private equity is about more than capital. It's about transformation—turning companies, industries, and markets into something better. That power comes with a responsibility to think beyond quarterly earnings and focus on the long-term health of the economy and society."

Griffiths envisions an industry that drives innovation, creates sustainable value, and leads with purpose. "The next decade will reward those who embrace change and prioritize building something that lasts."

The Path Ahead

The private equity industry's next chapter will not be written solely in boardrooms or balance sheets. It will be defined by how firms adapt to a world that is more interconnected, more conscious, and more demanding of accountability. The opportunity to lead is immense, but it requires bold action and a willingness to break with tradition.

The challenges are significant: geopolitical uncertainty, evolving regulatory landscapes, and the need to address systemic issues like climate change and inequality. Yet, these same challenges present opportunities to innovate, grow, and redefine what private equity can achieve.

A Call to Lead

The time to act is now. Private equity has the tools, expertise, and influence to lead transformational change. By aligning financial success with social responsibility, the industry can shape a future where profit and progress go hand in hand.

"This is private equity's moment," Griffiths concludes. "The question isn't whether we can rise to meet the challenges of our time—it's whether we will. The decisions we make today will define our legacy tomorrow."

The future of private equity is one of possibilities. By embracing sustainability, leveraging technology, and committing to transparency, the industry can create lasting value—for investors, businesses, and society as a whole. The next decade is not just an opportunity for growth; it's a chance to lead with purpose.

Additional Resources for Further Reading

For readers who want to delve deeper into private equity, economic development, and the transformative forces shaping the industry, the following resources provide valuable insights:

Books

- **Private Equity: History, Governance, and Operations** by Harry Cendrowski
  A comprehensive overview of private equity, including its history, operational practices, and governance structures.
- **King of Capital: The Remarkable Rise, Fall, and Rise Again of Steve Schwarzman and Blackstone** by David Carey and John E. Morris
  An engaging narrative about the rise of one of the most successful private equity firms, offering insight into the industry's evolution.
- **Sustainable Investing: Revolutions in Theory and Practice** by Cary Krosinsky and Nick Robins
  A deep dive into the principles and applications of sustainable investing, with relevance to ESG-focused private equity.

Reports and Research

- **Preqin Global Private Equity Report** (Annual)
  A comprehensive review of trends, performance, and emerging opportunities in private equity.
- **McKinsey & Company: Private Markets Annual Review**
  Insights into private market performance, sector highlights, and emerging trends shaping the industry.
- **World Economic Forum: The Future of Private Equity**
  A forward-looking exploration of private equity's role in fostering sustainability, innovation, and economic growth.

Online Resources

- **Institutional Limited Partners Association (ILPA)**
  Resources on best practices, industry standards, and educational materials for private equity professionals.
  Website: www.ilpa.org
- **Emerging Markets Private Equity Association (EMPEA)**
  Research, data, and analysis on private equity activity in emerging markets.
  Website: www.empea.org
- **ESG and Private Equity (PRI)**
  The Principles for Responsible Investment (PRI) offers guidance on integrating ESG factors into private equity strategies.
  Website: www.unpri.org

Glossary of Terms

AUM (Assets Under Management) - The total market value of investments managed by a private equity firm or other financial institution.

Buyout - An acquisition strategy where a private equity firm purchases a controlling interest in a company, often with the goal of improving performance and selling at a profit.

Capital Call - A request by a private equity fund for investors to provide the capital they have committed, often used to finance acquisitions or operations.

Carried Interest - The share of profits that private equity fund managers earn as compensation, typically a percentage of the fund's profits above a certain threshold.

Direct Alpha - A performance measurement tool that compares the cash flows of private market investments to a public market benchmark to assess value creation.

Due Diligence - The comprehensive process of evaluating a potential investment's financial, operational, and market risks before making a decision.

ESG (Environmental, Social, and Governance) - Criteria used to evaluate a company's ethical impact and sustainability practices, increasingly integrated into investment strategies.

GP (General Partner) - The private equity firm managing the fund, responsible for making investment decisions and managing operations.

IRR (Internal Rate of Return) - A metric used to evaluate the profitability of an investment, representing the discount rate that makes the net present value of all cash flows equal to zero.

LP (Limited Partner) - An investor in a private equity fund, typically institutional entities like pension funds, endowments, or sovereign wealth funds.

Portfolio Company - A company in which a private equity fund has invested.

Secondaries - The buying and selling of pre-existing investor commitments to private equity funds.

Vintage Year - The year in which a private equity fund begins operations or makes its first investment, often used to compare fund performance.

www.ingramcontent.com/pod-product-compliance
Lightning Source LLC
Chambersburg PA
CBHW070110230526
45472CB00004B/1207